MW00933926

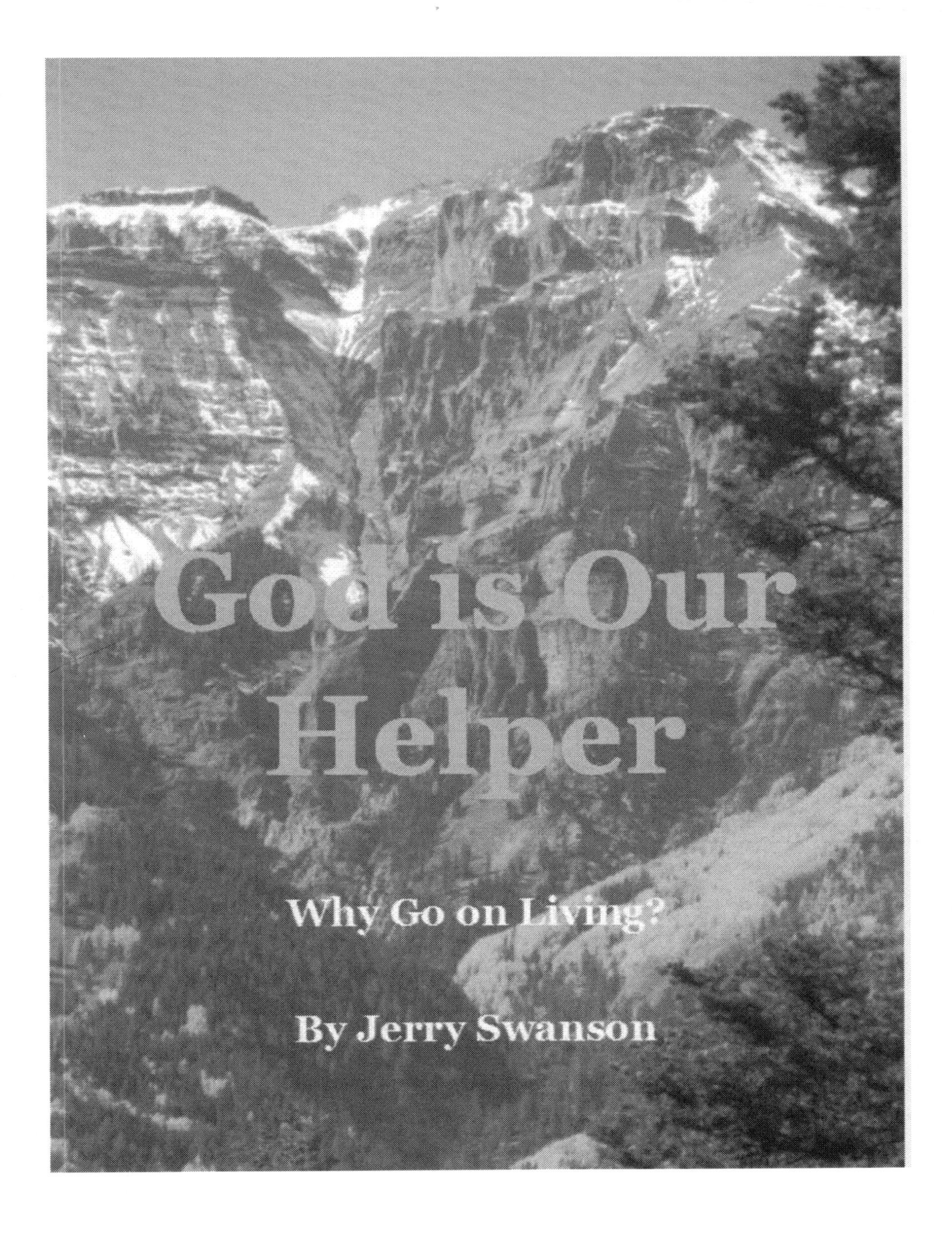
God is Our
Helper
Why Go on Living?
By Jerry Swanson

God is Our Helper

Why go on living?

Written by Jerry Swanson

Front cover: This picture was taken in our favorite place to vacation; Ouray, Colorado.

Back cover: This picture of Jerry and Donna Swanson was taken in New York state, near the finger lakes region, on our 50th honeymoon.

ISBN-13: 978-1539941224

ISBN-10: 1539941221

BISAC: Christian Living

Printed in the United States of America

Table of Contents

"For God so loved the world that He gave His only Son, so that everyone who believes in Him will not perish but have eternal life. God did not send His son into the world to condemn it, but to save it. There is no judgment awaiting those who trust Him.

But those who do not trust Him have already been judged for not believing in the only Son of God." John 3:16-18

Dedication and Introduction

Picture of Jerry and Donna

Independence Pass, Colorado

Donna and I dedicate this book to those who are seeking a God who cares and who can be trusted. This is our God. I, Jerry, also dedicate this book to my beloved wife Donna who has been my helper, a true angel of God, for over 50 years.

Jerry and Donna Kay Swanson live in Loveland, Colorado with their wonderful children and grandchildren whom they cherish, and blessed by God by many friends near and far.

You will be able to see the hand of God in our lives we went through good times and hard times like everyone and yet we keep trusting God and God leads us in His path. We are simply ordinary people with an extraordinary God and savior in Jesus Christ.

We encourage all to consider God and then to completely trust God. The devil wants us to distrust God and drift from His ways, and to lose the firm foundation of God and His wisdom.

While living in Seattle, we attended a marriage enrichment event that sealed a vision for our life when asked to write and ponder the question "why do you want to go on living?".

The title of the book is The Lord is our Helper, taken from 1 Samuel 7:12 after the prophet had cried out to God for help in the face of great disaster and God helped Samuel. He set memorial called "Ebenezer".

"My plans are good for you "says God, "not for evil but for a good future" . Jeremiah 29:11

God's book, the Bible, has 1000s of promises to those who will put their trust in Him, we pray that you will seek this God and all that He has in store for you.

"The Lord is a shelter for the oppressed, a refuge in times of trouble. Those who know Your name trust in You, for You, O Lord, have never abandoned anyone who searches for You." Psalms 9:9

The richest man in the World, saved by mercy of God, and being refined and re-fired. There is nothing that has happened in my life, but that God does deserve all the Glory. He is the faithful One.

Jerry Swanson

Purpose of the book

1. To thank family and friends for their faithfulness.
2. To thank God for His mercy and faithfulness.
3. To share the vision for our life, "Why go on living"?
4. To bless you, the reader, with hope in God to help you.
5. To honor God by sharing stories of His goodness 70 years.
6. To provide a record for family and friends.
7. To share the mistakes I have made - hoping others avoid.
8. To encourage couples to be steadfast in their marriage.
9. To share simple steps that made a difference in our marriage.
10. To celebrate the life of Donna Kay and me together.
11. To share the secret to a successful life made know to all.
12. To share our hope of the last days and life forever in heaven.

"For this is the secret; Christ lives in you and this is your assurance that you will share in his Glory". Col 1:27

1. God's plans are good

"For I know the plans I have for you," says the Lord. "They are plans for good and not for disaster, to give you a future and a hope". Jeremiah 29:11

God helps in growing up days

The boy from Nebraska

It was in the hills of northern Nebraska where Phyllis Ilene Esau Swanson lived and reared my sister Judie and me, while my father, Ray, served his country in the Army. Phyllis gave birth to me on December 5, 1944 on what was probably a very cold winter day in Osceola, Nebraska.

In 1945, my father was coming back from the war, so my mother drove to Texas to pick him up. On the way back, they had a flat tire on the highway and while my father fixed the tire on the narrow road, two trucks passed and hit each other. Our car went tumbling down into the ditch below. Both me and my sister, Judie, who was a couple of years older than me, were asleep in the back seat. My mother ran down to the car and was grateful to find us alive and okay. God was our helper.

My mother was a godly woman who served God and the family and others in need with an unselfish heart and had a strong faith, praying for many. She was a peacemaker. She always had faith in God. She also had faith in me and lifted me up even when I made mistakes. She became ill after I left home and died after a brave battle with cancer in January of 1966.

My father was a very religious man and a good husband and father. He was a man of integrity and loved by many. He was hard working. The family lived on the farm in Northeast Nebraska until a tornado came and destroyed the house and barns and livestock. So my parents moved to Lincoln where my father delivered Omar bread in trucks. Later the family moved to Grand Island and dad started his television business.

While my parents lived in Lincoln, they were contacted by a man named Frank Driver who introduced Jesus to them. They attended a church in Lincoln with Preacher Hershel Dyer, and I remember how our family ministered to others including a blind man that needed a ride to church. My family was hospitable, showing kindness to many. We later moved to Grand Island.

God helped our family many times--especially as we would visit grandparents on their farms in the hills of northern Nebraska. We flew across those dirt hills at what seemed high speeds, in our 1955 green-and-white Ford station wagon. Whoa!

These are good memories of the farms with grandparents and kin. I can recall one time when Dad, the cowboy, helped his brothers when they could not control a wild horse. Dad just went out and rode it with ease. My Grandpa Elmer organized the Swanson Rodeo each year in Central City, Nebraska. My dad loved to ride in the rodeo.

My other grandpa was Charley Esau. At his farm, my brother Rod and I were playing on the haystacks (round bales). Rod slipped down between the bales and was shouting for help. God helped as I finally walked over and saw him and pulled him out. Rod shares that story to this day. God is faithful and has always taken care of us.

We had many good times on Grandpa Charley's farm. I loved the chores of bringing the water bucket in from the windmill, and bringing the corncobs and coal for the stove in the living room during the winter. I also remember sitting around the table at night, a kerosene lantern lighting the room, with the glowing faces of my family around the table, and listening to the stories. It seemed that everyone was talking at once.

We always attended church and trusted God. At the age of twelve, I was leading worship in our a cappella singing church, and the preacher's wife would always "take over" with her loud voice. I lived for the day I could "out sing" her and truly lead. I was bashful as a boy, but grew strong in faith in God and service to others with encouragement from my parents.

I was blessed with an older sister Judie, with brother Rod (five years younger), and little sister Rona (10 years younger). They all have grown and have families now--we love each other a lot.

Growing up with my brother and sisters taught us how to give and take. I remember the "can-can days" (they were big undergarments that the girls wore). My older sister would fuss about her can-can. As she sat in the back seat on the way to church, she would say, "don't touch my skirt." That was pretty hard since it was huge and took over most of the seat.

All my memories of my brother and sisters, and family are good.

From left to right - Brother Rod, Sister Judie, Jerry in middle with Rona on lap, Father Ray, Mother Phyllis. Rona holds black cuddly Puddles who made puddles when patted.

One morning at breakfast, the family was talking, and as I heard what they were talking about, I said, “What fire?” The family stared at me, and then realized that I had slept through the fire during the night. The garage had burnt down and the fire trucks had come and put out the fire. I never woke up, and fortunately, being sound sleep was okay since the fire did not jump into the house. My bedroom was right next to the garage.

While a young teenager, I appreciated my father involving me in church matters, such as the business meeting to discuss church matters.

I remember the time that the church was $125 short of what they needed to pay bills. The men prayed and then each offered extra money to get things back on course. I learned quickly to trust in God.

Life has problems. There was a church member who was very hard to get along with. I went with my dad to visit this man at his home; he met us at the door with a shotgun. My dad simply said, “We came to talk with you and pray, not to fight,” and the man cooperated. I learned a lot from observing my father.

When we had church potlucks, my mom told our family to wait until all had eaten to see if there was enough left for us. I remember when Norvin Dunagan offered to bring beef from his farm so we could have a steak fry. It was amazing how fast the church grew upon that announcement. People came from all around. God helps at potlucks too.

During my teen years, my best friend in school, Ben Welch, helped me get a paper route. So each day after school we would head to the paper company, get our papers, and deliver them. I remember:

- Delivering in the cold snow days while I could smell dinner at each of the 114 homes.
- Trying to collect the 35-cent weekly fee on Saturdays for the paper delivery and how some people did not or could not pay.
- The older lady who could not afford so she paid with a sack of fresh rolls on Saturday. I would take them home to my mother.

That was my first experience at small business and dealing with customers, that being all types of people.

We kids were taught to focus on serving others and not ask for money. Seems I did well at that most of my life, but is funny how money shows the true character of people. I remember knocking at a house to collect my 35 cents and hearing the people leave out the back door to avoid me.

My extended family members showed me kindness including both grandparents: Elmer and Marie Swanson on my dad's side and Charley Roy and Anna Lou Esau on my mother's side. Others who showed me kindness included my cousin Phillip with Emily Esau, Uncle Ted and Aunt Betty, Uncle Vernon and Aunt Arlene Swanson with daughter Susan, and Aunt Rosalie with husband Don "Red".

When adults show interest in young people it can make a big impact on their lives, and I pray that I might also show kindness to the young people whose lives I touch.

One day, my parents took us kids to visit Vernon and Arlene who lived on a farm south of Lincoln. Once released from the car, my brother Rod and I went to look around the farm, and in the process found an old rusty can of beer. We decided to go into the silo and check it out. We had taken care to lock the door. Just then someone jerked the door and our dad loudly said, "Jerry, are you in there? Unlock the door!"

I was looking for a place to put that can of beer that we had just opened, and that we were not supposed to have. As I looked up, I saw an opening in the silo wall. So I gave it a fling. As it went up, the beer was squirting all over and then it hit the walls and made a lot of racket all the way down.

Gaining composure, I opened the door.

You could smell beer, but nothing was said except I did not dare look at dad. Vernon led us around the farm for a while and as Vernon and dad got ready to go to the house, Vernon casually mentioned, "Guys, if you see any rusty pop or beer cans around here, I would not bother them. They might not be good. Thanks Vernon for the gentle leading.

In my teen years, I worked for my father at Swanson's TV and Appliance business at Five Point in Grand Island. We (me and Ben Welch my High School friend) would help put up TV antennas, long before cable. It was in those days that black and white TV eventually advanced to color TV. Color TV was very marginal in quality for several years before you actually could see distinct colors.

We had two family vacations growing up; one to California to see my mother's sister, Darlene Dunkle and family. We drove straight through as a family of six could not afford stopping along the way. While visiting the Dunkles we go to go see the Rose Parade early in the morning.

The other trip was to Colorado. One of the special memories in Colorado was a drive up Phantom Canyon where a thunderstorm had washed out a bridge so we had to turn around in the storm on a mountain ledge and go home. My dad always remembered that canyon drive. I remembered Colorado. It has always held my heart ; the Rocky Mountains, the stream, and the adventure.

An even far better adventure has been my life with Jesus., It was a blessing to be brought up in a church environment with a sincere love of God and reverence for His Word. Jesus became my friend.

Jerry's high school picture

The Girl from Kansas

God was surely designing one of His treasured people when He brought Donna Kay into the precious home of Park and Hollis Smith on June 3, 1944. It was on a warm summer day in central Kansas, and somewhere out there, in another place, her someday love, had not yet been born (that's me).

Donna Kay's name means "beautiful lady, joyous life". Ruth 3:11 says: "blessed are you virtuous woman–light and life of God." Truly God created a cherished treasure in this lady.

Donna Kay was six years old when her much-older sister Betty married Allen Keeler on a terribly hot June day—so hot that the taper candles were melting and had to be extinguished during the ceremony. Donna was very disappointed when Allen and Betty didn't take her with them as they departed for their honeymoon in that green '49 Chevy.

Putnam C16 School District had a little one-room schoolhouse where Donna Kay attended school, and she was delighted to learn. Her world expanded as she was exposed to the personalities of the other students.

Her wonderful teacher was Mrs. Adams. Donna Kay listened and learned as the teacher worked with older pupils. Donna enjoyed most subjects and did well....except for reading comprehension–she still felt insecure with that!

Donna Kay in front of her prairie home, Stafford, Kansas built by her father, Park

In fair weather, recess found her class divided into two teams for softball. The teacher could hit that ball really far! Donna and her school mates practiced for the spring track meet competition with several other county schools. Inclement weather found Donna Kay and her classmates around the piano with Mrs. Adams' fingers cascading up and down the keyboard while the kids sang. They all loved Mrs. Adams.

Attending church every time possible was another important socialization for Donna Kay. The country church building was nine miles from home, so on Sunday evening, on the way to church, the car radio was tuned to Fibber McGee and Molly and Amos 'n Andy-- a happy time.

God's Word was implanted in her heart and mind from earliest memories. Yet, try as she would to stay alert and listen, Donna would nod, lean, and end up asleep, usually in her mom's lap. Singing inspired her and it was there in the Bethel church that she learned to read music and to harmonize. She says "Thank You, Lord, for that joy".

Donna Kay growing up in Kansas fourth grade

Donna's brother "Sonny", who was 13 years older, chose not to attend college. Instead, he stayed to help Donna's dad with ranching and farming. The Smiths worked hard to live a quiet life amongst the salt marshes of what is now known as Quivera Wildlife Refuge northeast of Stafford. Donna was twelve when they had to move. The move was caused due to the government takeover for protection of the migratory birds. Today there remains a sign posted Park Smith Pond.

It was a difficult time for all the local families because their community was being dispersed. Families who'd lived in the area for generations were suddenly forced with relocation. Donna's family moved to a farm near Nickerson, Kansas. Sonny remained on the home place overseeing the livestock on rented government property, until they said, "Out".

He moved to where his parents were living, and together they all got to meet, know, and love the new church family in Hutchinson. He blessed "L'il Sis" by transporting her to youth gatherings—mostly for a soda after church somewhere. A very special person throughout those teen years in the church was Linda Young, the oldest of five daughters. Linda was an avid reader, smart, expressive, an influencer. Donna was insecure with her at first, but Linda became a true friend and remains so to this day.

Donna's parents, Park and Hollis, set an example of living a godly life that set the course for Donna's life of upright character and respect for others. Hospitality to family and strangers was common. They always had enough, raising cows including milk cows, pigs, chickens, and, at one time, catfish. Life was good, but there was always work to do. For example, during her high school years, her summer job was helping a farm couple watch their kids and preparing meals so that they could both do field work.

One incident stands out in Donna's young life. The eight-mile trip home from school in a blizzard was long. About thirty other people ended up stranded at their house. Her mother made a big pot of chili and all stayed safe and warm at the Smiths' home until the storm cleared. The Lord helped her family, and as God helped them, they in turn helped others.

Her father was one of the most honorable men that I ever knew. He never endured gossip and he walked humbly with God. He was upright in how he treated others. The following scriptures reflect His life.

> *"Pure and lasting religion in the sight of God our Father means that we must care for orphans and widows in their troubles, and refuse to let the world corrupt us." James 1:27.*
>
> *"The godly walk in integrity; blessed are their children after them" Proverbs 20:7.*

As I write this, I am thankful to God for Donna's godly parents and good friends Linda Young Wheeler and Janie Stiggins Colle. They both were a positive influence, God took care of Donna Kay as she grew up to be a true woman after His heart, very beautiful, inside and out.

As you look back at her life and study her today, you know God developed in her character traits of Jesus as a kind and loving person. She has great respect and patience for all, and is an unselfish and competent servant.

Through good teaching at home and in church, and by reading her Bible, Donna Kay learned to stay on the good path God had for her and to make choices that were true, pure, and honest.

Perhaps you did not have honorable parents, and there is pain and bad memories from your childhood. I am truly grieved that happened to you, and I pray you will allow God to heal those hurts.

May you find strength in the love of our great Father God who calls us as His children to come home and into the arms. His love for you is amazing and sure. Luke 15

Donna trusted God and found him always faithful just as I did growing up and God has helped both Donna and me throughout our lives as we keep seeking after Him and receiving his Fatherly love.

Donna Kay as Freshman at York College

Do you know my Jesus?

God sent His Son Jesus to live a life for us to follow, to die for our sins, and to set us free and give us His Spirit of power, love, and wisdom to empower us to be victorious. This is the message of the New Testament. Every word is true.

I have two loves in my life: Jesus and Donna Kay.

Jesus is the Good Shepherd and He takes care of His sheep. Jesus said "I am the gate. Those who come in through me will be saved. Wherever they go, they will find green pastures. The thief's purpose is to steal and kill and destroy. My purpose is to give life in all its fullness. " John 10:9-10

Both Donna Kay and I know Jesus and have followed Him for fifty years together. We have continued to read and re-read, and to follow His Holy Word and seek His help, and to welcome His Holy Spirit. Life is lived one day at a time with the Lord's help. He is faithful to help us day by day.

We are very ordinary folk with nothing to boast except of God's mercy.

Donna and I stand together in honoring our God and we rejoice in His care. He is faithful indeed. We also know that God calls us His children and loves us with all His heart. We find it amazing to know such a God— this God of ours and yours– will do anything to rescue us and restore us as His children.

God of the Old Testament was exacting and when someone sinned, they paid the penalty, even death. But God made a new covenant in His Son Jesus to show His great mercy.

> *"For the mountains may depart and the hills disappear, but even then I will remain loyal to you. My covenant of blessing (kindness) will never be broken, says the Lord, who has mercy on you. Your enemies will always be defeated because I am on your side. I have created the blacksmith who fans the coals beneath the forge and makes the weapons of destruction. And I have created the armies that destroy. But in the coming day, no weapon formed against you will succeed. And everyone who tells lies in court will be brought to justice. These benefits are enjoyed by the servants of the Lord; their vindication will come from Me, I, the Lord have spoken". Isaiah 54:10, 15–17*

God's gift to us is Jesus, and life in Him sets us free when we believe and receive Him and follow Him. Salvation is a free gift, and we can do nothing to obtain our salvation. It is a gift–Hallelujah!

Without the shed blood of Christ Jesus, that is Jesus the Lamb of God, dying for our sins, we could never close the gap between the righteousness of God and our frail lives of failure (we are "toast" without His mercy). But then Jesus came to earth and lived a pure and perfect life, He suffered incredibly, then died for you and me to set us free from sin and to give us eternal life.

But that's not the end of the story, because then He rose from the tomb to give us victory forever and ever.

> *"But God is so rich in mercy, and He loved us so much, that even while we were dead because of our sins, He gave us life when He raised Christ from the dead. It is only by God's special favor that you have been saved. God saved you by His special favor when you believed. And you can't take credit for this; it is a gift of God. For we are God's masterpiece. He has created us anew in Christ Jesus, so that we can do good things he planned for us long ago." Ephesians 2:4-5, 8-9, 10*

You may say, "I am too messed up. God could never forgive me." Well, we are all messed up. You may not know it, but Jesus created you unique, and He is in the business of making a new person out of each of us who believe in Him. He can do it as we trust Him and follow the instructions in His book—the Bible–one step at a time.

You may say, "I do not need God." You are wrong. Sooner or later you will find that you need Him. Sooner or later you will realize that nothing matters in this world compared to loving God and following Him. God and Jesus are as one, and the Holy Spirit is a gift to help us live an honorable life for Him and with Him.

Do you know my Jesus?

If you do not know Him, please accept His love for you today and become His friend and follow His ways. Pray that God will show you a church family that truly loves God and proclaims Jesus and His ways. Continue to read His Word for instruction. Begin with John or Mark to show you the way, and go on to Acts and obey what God asks you to do. God bless you indeed. Become a follower of Jesus and walk the walk.

2. God's Help brought us together

"Whatever is good and perfect comes to us from God above, who created all heavens' lights. Unlike them, He never changes or casts shifting shadows." James 1:17

God helps in college and marriage

Jerry and Donna . . . Could it be?

The Lord's plans were good for us as we entered York College in the Fall of 1962. Both of us were busy with school and other activities, including intramural sports, cheerleading for Donna Kay, and a job for me.

Our first verbal interaction was on a winter evening in the cafeteria where a few students were playing Hearts. Donna Kay was there to get ice and I asked her to join our table. She didn't know the game but surely would enjoy the company! HEARTS opening...

Jerry and Donna Kay on their first big date.

Later in February, the school had their big event, the Sweetheart Banquet. I assumed that Donna Kay had a date, but heard she had not taken the invite of others, so I asked and she accepted and that was the beginning of our relationship.

We spent time together as often as we could. Our common activities involved church and choir. I worked at Ace Drive Inn and occasionally smuggled a burger and fries into the dorm for my girl.

Jerry working at the Ace Drive Inn

Being in the choir was a major highlight of the YC (York College) experience for both of us. As important as notes, harmony, and timing of music pieces were, our director emphasized the spiritual meaning...instruction for our souls–the wonderful hymns about Jesus.

The Spring Tour and other weekend performances allowed us not only to sing and give glory to God, but also to enjoy the hospitality of the church and individuals/families in whose homes we stayed. The director, Joe Lewis and his wife Mary, were godly people who taught us reverence and joy in the Lord.

I wrote love notes to Donna Kay and suggest that we go to Colorado someday after we married, get a cabin, and raise a family.

At the end of our first year, we made a mistake at the dare of one of the couples who were friends. We snuck out after curfew and stayed out all night. It was a foolish youthful decision which, when we were caught, brought shame to our parents and probation for the next school year. We were both very sorry for being foolish in making that mistake, and we never did anything like that again. Breaking the rules intentionally doesn't help us develop our character, causes us to take unnecessary chances, and doesn't glorify God.

During the following summer, we had limited communication as I was busy working and Donna was working with a farm family. And, as we look back we can see how the hand of God kept us together.

Fortunately, in the fall of the next year, we both returned to York, and once the administration observed our repentant attitudes and good behavior, we were extended trust by the faculty once again. God helped us as we resumed our relationship and our activities at York.

Donna also came back to Grand Island with me and was able to meet my family who all loved her immediately. I knew that if my mother liked Donna Kay, she was "a go". I call them both "angels on earth".

God was looking after us and helping us, but also trying to protect us from harm physically or spiritually. We both believed in Jesus with all our heart and sought to be wise.

Sometimes when we are about to make a big decision, we want God's approval or direction. When two young people are in love, the emotions sometime overcome their minds. It was a blessing to have godly parents and family praying for us.

At York College, Donna Kay went with me to Central City on Sundays where I led the songs, preached, prayed, and did communion for my Grandmother Swanson and a few others. It was a small but precious church. We enjoyed serving the Lord and others together. The Lord helped us.

As you consider who to marry, it is wise to take time to observe how each of you are careful to honor your parents and others before marriage. In doing so, you can better understand the other person's character, habits, and attitudes. Remember that your goal is to live with this person for the rest of your life. What might be a small irritant now will surely expand to a major frustration. Do not assume that the person you are thinking of marrying will all of a sudden be a much better person after marriage. Seek God's guidance in all things.

Pray together for wisdom. A sure sign of maturity is a person's willingness to receive correction upon confrontation with love and truth. If a person remains defensive, indifferent, or simply unloving, then you need to wait and pray for a change of heart.

Staying in the assembly of godly believers is vital. If one just listens to advice from those who are standing in sin, then they will get bad advice to do whatever feels good rather than what God wants. Be wise and follow God. Read the Word of God together and live.

Yet one thing remains when two love each other in purity before the Lord. It is so sweet and precious. One of my favorite memories was picking lilacs for Donna. There was something about the fragrance of the flower blending with the fragrance of this beautiful lady and love that created a sweet perfume.

There were many people who were instrumental in helping Donna Kay and me court, and who made our years in York College more enjoyable. Joel White, a fun-loving Christian roommate and friend, loaned me his car for dates with Donna Kay. Larry Brewster, my sister Judie's husband, occasionally lent his car to us. Dickie Hill helped me in tennis. And where would we be without our patient professors and the university staff, or Loren Swanson (Swany) who hired me at Ace Drive Inn.

God helped me through life, but He used many people as His hands and feet.

God is the fountain–She said "yes"

It was April '64 when I took Donna for a walk in Grand Island near my parents' home. There was a lake in the park, a perfect and quiet setting for what I was about to do. I asked Donna Kay to marry me and offered her the engagement ring I had bought especially for her. I loved to buy her dresses, and she was wearing a yellow dress I'd chosen for her. She was beautiful.

I did not know that I was supposed to talk to her father first to get permission before I asked Donna Kay, even though her father knew me.

So Donna Kay simply said, "Yes, but I need to talk to my parents." She did, and they were supportive. Fortunately, I had spent enough time with her parents that they had confidence in me as their daughter's future husband.

It was a tradition at York College for any young lady who got engaged to have a special way to announce it during the evening devotions in the girls' dorm. Someone who knew the secret would begin singing the beautiful song, "God is the Fountain Whence", and all the students would look around to see who was now engaged. Someone else lit a candle, then the song began, and once the secret was revealed, the candle was extinguished.

Part of the proposal from me to Donna Kay was the announcement that I intended to continue my education and work in Colorado, and I wanted her to go with me. I was trusting entirely in God to help us. I knew it was a huge risk for Donna Kay to trust not only God but also this young man she had grown to love.

Once engaged, our relationship took on a more mature perspective of planning and preparing. We were very much in love, and also had a lot to get done in a short period of time.

After school was over, Donna Kay traveled with my family to deliver me to Denver where I would get established. Homer Wolfe was the director of Denver Tech

School where I would study, and he recommended a pastor and wife team, Bob and Billie Woods, as a place to stay.

When we arrived with my family at the Woods' home after a long drive from Colorado, they invited us in for tacos--something we never had eaten in Nebraska but sure did enjoy. We kind of thought that we would be spending a few days together before Donna Kay and my family had to get back home.

I was not prepared for what was about to happen.

My father called me outside and said, "I have given the Woods the money for rent for this month and so we will need to leave tonight and go back. I have no more money to rent a motel and stay any longer." I had hoped to spend a little time together, especially for Donna and me. Then my father took off his watch and gave it to me. "I want you to have this."

I then called Donna outside and told her the sad news, and we kissed each other, and it was really hard to see her leave that night with my family to return to Grand Island. When she got back, her parents met them her at my parents' house and took her home to Kansas for the summer while I got established in Denver.

When they left, I went inside the house and sat down to talk to Bob and Billie. Every time they asked me a question, a big lump came up into my throat and I could not speak, so I said, "Please excuse me while I retire for the night." They had a nice little bed in the unfinished basement, along with a shower, and that is where I spent most of my summer quietly working and going to school.

I remember lying in bed that night and praying fervently for the safe travel of my family back home, and my beloved Donna Kay. I remember seeing a vision of angels over that car all the way home. God helped and so did His angels.

The next day I started to walk across Denver to find a job because I didn't have a car. I walked for miles checking with different restaurants, drawing on the experience I had working as a cook in York. During that day, I stopped at a bicycle shop and purchased a used 10-speed bike for $35. That would be my transportation around Denver for both work and school each day.

As I sat down that evening for dinner with Bob and Billie, someone was at the door. Mr. Evans came by from Evans Diner and asked if I would like a job. He took me in his car to the restaurant and explained the details.

So I accepted the job offer, and started work the next day by going to the restaurant at 4:00 a.m. and working until about 2:00 p.m., and then going home for a short nap before heading out to school from 7:00 p.m., and back home about 10:00 p.m. God helped. My 10-speed bike took me everywhere.

I attended the church where Bob was the preacher, at Logan Street Church. I worked hard and went to school. Later in the summer, I rode the train back to Grand

Island where my dad helped me purchase my first car. It was a 1959 mint green Oldsmobile. It served us well. God helped and Dad helped.

Donna Kay and her mother Hollis came to visit me during the summer and somehow God helped me find a cute little apartment. Donna and her mom stayed with me and visited. Before they came, I wasn't sure if I was going to be able to spend much time with them, but they came anyway, and it was a wonderful treat for me to see them. Later the owners of that apartment allowed us to have a bigger apartment if we would oversee the place. There were several older ladies who lived in the apartments and we all shared a common bath. It worked.

God was so faithful during that summer, to help Donna back home, and me in Denver in preparation for our new life together. We stand and praise His name.

"What God has joined together" – Jerry and Donna

Donna Kay and I were joined together before God, family, and friends on the evening of September 4, 1964 in Hutchinson, Kansas at the Church of Christ. I arrived the night before from Denver with Joel White. Donna Kay had Janie Colle and Linda Wheeler stand with her, while I was blessed to have Joel White and Ben Welch as best men. Preacher Duane Eggleston performed a lovely service. Donna's dear parents and friends, and my parents, family, and friends all made sure it was a beautiful wedding and party. It was a precious time. My mother Phyllis had cancer at the time and wasn't feeling well, but she pushed through and made the special for everybody.

There was a gathering time and a beautiful cake. Then as Donna was changing clothes and pictures were taken, Joel drove the Olds around in front of the church. So Donna and I ran to the car through a shower of flying rice and well wishes.

Jerry and Donna at their wedding in Hutchinson, Kansas.

Wedding party from left Karen Keeler, Janie Stiggins, Ben Welch back, Rona Swanson front, Linda Wheeler,

John Smith back, Donna Kay, Duane Eggleston minister in back, Jerry Swanson, Kimberly Keeler flower girl, Tom Higdon, Joel White and Rod Swanson. May God bless all who were in our wedding.

We left and headed for Colorado, a little tired but ready to begin our life together. However, I regret that it did not dawn on me to go say goodbyes to our parents. We were caught up in the moment of excitement and just went on our way--the emotions of youth.

When we came to our little apartment in Denver, I went back to work and Donna got settled in our apartment. Then my boss gave me a few days off for our honeymoon. We had a modest honeymoon as we took off to the mountains, exploring mountain roads and hiking and just loving each other.

There was a road that we took behind Mt. Elbert and we went for a walk in the mountains and it began raining. When we returned to the car, the keys were dangling in the ignition with the doors locked. Donna Kay was able to take a branch and somehow, with the help of God, fish the keys out an opening in the window. Thank you, beloved Donna Kay, and thank you, God.

Several weeks after settling in Denver, we took time to call our parents and say hello. I seem to recall it went something like, "Sorry for not being more thoughtful." My dad said "we could not find you that night of the wedding and we thought you would stay with us at the farm for a couple nights".

Back in Denver, God helped us with a place to stay, and a precious little church on Logan Street where we had the friendship of another young couple named Jim and Ann Thompson from Arkansas. One day they took us "camping" on Sugar Loaf Mountain. They had two sleeping bags and they took one and gave us one--our first-time experience. It was amazing that when you're young and in love, the details really don't matter. We just made do.

Donna Kay has always loved children and worked with children in church and so one day she invited a couple with their child to our house to dinner. In those days, we might have a couple things in the refrigerator and a couple things on the shelf. So, we had some chili soup. My father always said "Offer what you have, do not fret." But the young mother who was our guest said, "My daughter and I do not like chili soup," so Donna offered them the only thing else we had which was beef and barley soup.

God helped us by giving us an apartment house to oversee in downtown Denver. It allowed us to get free rent. It was also an education on people in the big city as tenants would come and go. We met some interesting people. I meanwhile had jobs as a cook. Then one winter I sold Watkins door to door—items like pure vanilla and pepper. Then later I was blessed with a construction job at a block factory and made big money--$100 per week.

We could buy 3 dozen eggs for $1 and 3 pounds of hamburger for $1, bread for 5 cents, and gas for 17 cents a gallon. Things have changed a little bit over 50 years together.

We loved each other. We never had any special training on marriage or raising kids, just a simple faith in God. We were blessed as Donna Kay became pregnant. Thank you Lord, the giver of life.

During that time, I began working at Samsonite luggage. There was an accident at work--an explosion of caustic solution from a cleaning tank went into my eyes and my face and splashed parts of body. God helped, and the Superintendent took me to an eye specialist before going to the hospital and they were not sure if I would see again, and they wrapped my eyes.

It was during those two weeks that Donna would come and visit me in the hospital. I had stinky caustic all over my face and my body where there were some third-degree burns. God was so good to allow all the caustic to drop off and give me new skin.

Praise God! When they removed the wrappings around my eyes I could see. To this day, I praise God for excellent sight.

Thank you to an elderly couple from church, who allowed Donna to stay with them near the hospital for those two weeks.

When the Superintendent took me down town for my eye exam he said, "can you get out and wait for me while I park the car?" I was standing alone in downtown Denver with no clothes and only a wool blanket around me waiting as the superintendent parked the car.

I kept remembering one of the songs we sang in York Choir;

"Thou wilt keep him in perfect peace whose mind I stayed on thee,"
taken from Isaiah 26:3.

I had total peace the entire time. God helped again by completely healing me and giving me a wonderful life. At 70 years of age today, God still blesses me with good eyesight.

My parents came to visit us in Colorado in the fall of 1965. It was a chilly fall day, October 25, and we went to the mountains for a picnic. We did not realize that Colorado mountain terrain can turn into winter by late October, or even in September.

When people come to Colorado they expect to go the mountains, at least my dad did. So we found a place for a picnic on Rollinsville Road and huddled in our jackets. Then my dad was looking at the map and said, "Let's take that road up there going over the mountain in front of us".

We could see the clouds over the mountain but the sun was shining below, so off we went on an adventure. None of us had any clue to what lay ahead, nor did we have much mountain experience.

Believe it or not, we were about to go up a road that crossed a famous pass called Rollins Pass, an old railroad trestle rising up thousands of feet on the mountain side and we were driving the 1959 Oldsmobile.

When we came up the mountain and turned the corner, it was a snow storm and we were crossing that open trestle bridge. It was an adventure for my dad and terror for my mom and my wife. I was pretty scared, too. But God took care and brought us down the other side safely.

Later on, for our first anniversary, Donna and I went to the corner drug store as an outing, and on a whim, I looked over a bottle of wine. I was twenty years old at the time. I went to the counter and inquired about wine since I had never had any in my life, and the man asked to see my ID.

"ID, really?" Oops. Needless to say, we didn't buy the wine.

Later I graduated from Denver Technical School. IBM was located just a couple blocks from our apartment and so I applied for a job. After some tests and several visits, IBM hired me. Praise the Lord. I became a Service Representative in Denver. This was the beginning of a great thirty year career.

Thanking God Always

Thank You, Father, for your faithfulness to us during those early days. Thank you for bringing us together on the foundation of Jesus Christ and His Word. Thank you for providing, protecting, rescuing, and healing us. Thank You for keeping us on the right path. We give You all the glory and praise Your holy name. May our children and grandchildren also find You to be a faithful and loving God, and may all who seek You find You and walk in Your ways.

> *"Many sorrows come to the wicked, but unfailing love surrounds those who trust in the Lord. So rejoice in the Lord and be glad, all you who obey Him! Shout for joy, all you whose hearts are pure!" Psalms 32:10-11*

3. God is faithful in His time (Denver)

"There is a time for everything,
a season for every activity under heaven:
A time to be born and a time to die,
A time to plant and time to harvest,
A time to kill and a time to heal,
A time to tear down and a time to rebuild,
A time to cry and time to laugh,
A time to grieve and time to dance,
A time to scatter stones and a time to gather stones,
A time to embrace and a time to turn away,
A time to search and a time to lose,
A time to keep and a time to throw away,
A time to tear and time to mend,
A time to be quiet and a time to speak up,
A time to love and time to hate,
A time for war and time for peace."

Ecclesiastes 3:1-8

God helps in Denver as we begin a family

A time to be born - - Cherri and Wendy

God blessed Donna and me with a beautiful daughter named Cherri Kay on a snowy night at Porter Hospital in Denver, Colorado, on December 13, 1965.

Cherri's name came from Cherri Dunagan in Grand Island Church. Cherri's name means "beloved of God." Donna Kay and I have cherished Cherri all her life and thank God for this miracle in our lives. The name Kay means "full of joy."

Cherri has always had a strong spirit that has grown stronger in the Lord every year. When she was young, we remember when we were up late for an event, Cherri was right there with us. It might be midnight or 2 a.m.--she stayed up. When we went camping or on trips, she would roll with the activities--lots of energy. She is now a wonderful servant of the Lord, using her energy to bless her husband, family and others.

Life changes when children arrive. What a glorious blessing from God and what an awesome responsibility. God was faithful to us in blessing us with all we needed. The main thing was to trust God for help--love Cherri and take care of her.

Help came from Betsy Ward, a friend from church, who brought that first meal when we came home from the hospital with that "bundle of joy". Betsy (a young mother herself) was Donna's consultant regarding concerns as a young mother. Betsy and her husband Glenn became good friends, helping us along the way.

At University church during those early years, there were about 10 couples with one or more babies/toddlers—the nursery class was full! So, with training, the mothers took turns teaching these little ones. Donna still sings some of those first songs. Young mothers had their "pow-wows" to encourage each other and solve whatever parenting challenges were facing them at the time.

Donna and I lived in a one-bedroom apartment at 835 Sherman, and also managed the other seventeen apartments--a learning experience in human behaviors. God was surely with us.

One of the tenants at the apartment was a detective, seemingly a nice guy. However, one of the residents came to our door saying he saw the detective slit all our tires on our Olds. He said he saw him late at night as he came in the back of the building. So I went out and, sure enough, the tires were all flat. I went and confronted the detective but he denied it.

A potential renter came to check out an apartment one day; when Donna showed him the available one, the man said, "It won't work for me, as I need more room for all my wigs" Really ?

Donna's parents, Park and Hollis, would come and visit. Of course, everyone was excited to see the new little girl, Cherri. Grandparents are that way. Whenever Donna's parents came, they brought food from the farm. They also loved the mountains so we would go to the mountains and enjoy the creation of God. God was watching over us.

One day I received a letter from U.S. military inviting me to come and join them in the war in Viet Nam. I went to the Denver military facility, and went through the procedure and exams. As I sat with the officer in charge, I was on the verge of getting orders. Then I mentioned in our conversation our daughter Cherri.

Immediately the officer said, "If you have children you do not need to go." I said. "Sir, does that mean that I can leave now?" The officer said, "Yes".

My job at IBM included extensive six weeks training to fix Selectric typewriters. I was extremely blessed to have Donna's parents care for her while I was away. I was assigned a difficult territory in Denver with some of the toughest accounts in downtown Denver. I knew about getting up early, working hard, and taking full responsibility. Donna was faithful through all these changes and supportive of my work. We moved across town so I didn't need to commute so far, and to give us a little more living space.

We rented a two-bedroom apartment on Clayton, close to Washington Park. God blessed us with another cherished daughter on an early spring day at Porter Hospital. Wendy Lynn was born on March 22, 1967. What a blessing from heaven Wendy has been to us.

Wendy means "refreshing meadow and delight to God"–God our refuge of compassion. Her namesake was unique, cute little three-year-old Wendy Ward, Glenn and Betsy's first daughter. Wendy Lynn has always been a refreshing delight to both God and to us as parents, and to her husband and family.

Wendy loves the things of God: colors and flowers, music and rest (she did not fight nap or bedtime). She has a blend of both compassion and with the gift of speaking truth in gentleness. She is like a tender flower and also like a hardy plant that does not require too much care. She is a jewel, just as her sister Cherri is also.

Being parents was wonderful, but also a big responsibility.

Our good friends from church were Jerry and Judy Selby. During one of the times we were together, we talked about the idea of a backpack trip. So we went. Our destination was up a road off Hwy 285 on the way to Kenosha Pass.

We camped off a dirt road on the way to Wilson Peak. In those days I just loaded everything in a big pile and put black plastic around it, roped it up, and put it on my back. Hiking up the mountain, we found a level sheltered spot to set up camp for the night.

We went for a hike the next day. Jerry Selby and I climbed while Donna and Judy remained by the alpine lake. While hiking toward the crest, a rain cloud appeared with thunder and lightning bolts. The girls noticed their hair standing on end and, though funny, they realized they needed to get away from the lake. The lightning was too close for comfort! Down the mountain us guys came in a hurry and we thanked God for watching over all of us.

We would like to thank Delores and Jack Lewis for watching our beloved Cherri and Wendy while we took that special trip. They told us to pass that favor on to others. Getting-away time for couples is very important.

Donna Kay and I decided to venture out with the girls and go camping, so we purchased a canvas tent from Sears. We looked for a place on the map and found Bogan Flats near Marble.

Off we went in our little Volkswagen. After putting up the tent, we built a fire and cooked on an open fire–taco fixin's with hamburger, beans, and rice. Just about that time a storm came over the mountains, and we headed for the tent. It was a challenge with pots and pans, and the rain kept coming. It was a long night in the tent. I told creative stories to the girls. We survived our first campout.

Jerry and Donna with Cherri and Wendy.
Our first camping trip.

After that camping experience, I had a tarp made that came off the tent and had a couple poles so that we were prepared for the rain. To this day, putting up the tarp is the first thing that I do. Storms come quickly with little warning in the mountains of Colorado.

During our years while serving in University Church, I helped with devotions and led the singing. One of the couples came to me and actually offered to pay for me to go through seminary and be a preacher. I turned it down. Can you imagine? God bless them for the offer.

I had resolved that I wanted to be a Christian man that would experience the struggles of an ordinary businessman and build a Christian family with the help of God. Being a preacher was truly an honorable life, but it seemed that talking about living as a Christian was not as important as actually doing it. No offense to those that do preach.

IBM was looking for someone to move to Northern Colorado to take responsibility for the service in Greeley, Ft. Morgan, Wray, Holyoke, and Sterling areas, so they put out the word. They had several men interested in this job. I threw my name in the hat even though I had only worked for IBM one and half years. To my surprise, the manager called and asked if I wanted the job. I said, "Sure, but why me?" He said he had noticed my work and wanted me to take the job. So we moved to Greeley.

During our days at Greeley, we found a good church family, and rented a cute little house on 23rd near the University of Northern Colorado. We liked Greeley. It was more like a farm community—including the familiar smells!

Donna's parents came from Kansas to visit often, and we went camping together. Park liked to help me cut wood and build the fires, and Hollis helped with the cooking. Cherri and Wendy would get a stick and look through the woods. Donna and I still like to camp.

I served in the Boy Scouts with Ralph Bogart, who is my friend to this day. We remember good times at Boy Scout campouts, training up young men to respect God and country, to learn new skills, and to earn merit badges. Thank you, Ralph. We had a great time.

Donna was, and still is, a wonderful homemaker, mother, and wife. She always planted flowers and cared for them. Her home, no matter where, is filled with warmth and charm and neither I, nor our family, ever missed a meal. It was a tradition in our home to eat together as often as possible, to pray to God, to enjoy conversation, and to grow together.

God blessed me with the ability to speak, and I joined Toastmaster to improve that gift. Donna supported me in whatever I did, and she was right there with me when I won a regional speaking contest. Thank you for your support, beloved Donna. Glory be to God.

It was a privilege for me to work with IBM as a company founded on a Christian, Thomas Watson. In those days, the company hosted a family picnic in the summer and a family Christmas party in the winter. It was an exceptional company. I thank God for the honor.

While working in Greeley my boss called and said, "You have been carrying two territories and so we are going to train a new man and send him". I said. "Fine." Later they sent me a man who struggled with the preliminary testing and retook it several times but he had ambition and did not give up. IBM hired him with reservation and sent him to me.

Gene Balensiefen did a good job as he had ambition. He took to good training and instruction, and after one year, won the rookie of the year in IBM. Gene and June became good friends with Donna Kay and me. Along with their two sons, we camped together and helped each other.

Cherri and Wendy were pioneer babies, going wherever we went without hesitation. They went camping with us, to church with us, traveled with us. They are hardy to this day. They received lots and lots of love. I'm sure they made some mistakes, but I cannot honestly remember any.

Donna and I had a new little family now with Cherri and Wendy, and God had some new plans. It was hard to say good-bye for our next move.

There is a time to die - Phyllis Ilene "graduates"

Phyllis, my mother, had suffered for some time, and even at our wedding, she was ill. She was a true saint, always serving, never complaining. She was thinking about others and not herself. So, she died-- going to her home in heaven on January 16, 1966 on a cold day in Grand Island. She suffered greatly at the end of her days in the hospital from the cancer that had riddled her body, yet she prayed constantly for all her family.

Leading up to that day, Donna and I went home to visit Mom at the hospital (from Colorado to Grand Island). I remember seeing my dad sitting at the end of the hall, weary from the long path of seeing Mom gradually die. My dad was a great man, and did everything he could to help her through those days.

Another person was incredibly courageous and helpful for my mom during her days of suffering and pain was my sister, Judie, who had her own husband and children to care for. Still, she helped Dad, along with my siblings Rona and Rod who were still at home. Judie stood with Mom and was like a friend through those difficult times.

When Donna and I arrived to see my mom just before she died, she was her typical cheerful self, even though she was in very much pain. We prayed with her, as had Roger Hawley from York several times, and of course all the family. She prayed a special blessing on our little four week-old Cherri, which Cherri cherishes to this day.

A few things I remember about the funeral was sitting with my dad on the front row and singing "Face to face with Christ my Savior". Mom had a few favorites songs that I would lead for her and one of her special songs was "Lead me gently home Father" which God did.

At the funeral, many friends and family arrived. There were also several nurses from St. Francis Hospital that came. Surely, Mom had touched them with her love of Christ in all she did. She died with great courage and love for all. She was unselfish. Glory be to Jesus.

Memories of my mother are many: my mother singing a hymn while tears ran down her precious cheeks; her making us kids learn to do chores around the house, and do it well; her serving her parents, my grandparents, cleaning and cooking; her loving the little children that she taught at church, just like Donna Kay; always serving pleasant meals for the family and extended family. She loved to whistle, which delighted me since my beloved Donna does the same. I learned a lot from her, including making something of nothing, like tuna soup from a can of tuna and a milk. She loved the simple things of life, and she loved to talk about Jesus.

She was also a peacemaker.

There was a man in the church who was a troublemaker, and Mom sent him a letter encouraging peace. She did whatever was possible to build peace and harmony and work things out. Jesus Christ lived in her. She made a big difference.

On one of the trips back home before Mom died, Donna and I saw a very eerie sight. Most of our trips took place after I got off work at 5 p.m. on Friday and we would load the car and the kids, and off we went.

On a trip late at night as we entered Nebraska from Colorado, we came under a huge rain cloud that looked like it was threatening a downpour or a huge storm. Of course, that wasn't so unusual. And then to our right appeared a white rainbow, reminding us that God was there. We do not always understand all that happens or all that we see, but we can always trust God.

Here's a confession from me to my dear mother.

Over the years that I carried a paper route, I brought home, from time to time, a sack of the most delicious pastries. There were two of my favorite "long john" pastries--one with white coconut frosting and cream in the middle, and the other with caramel glaze and nuts on top. Both melted in your mouth.

Now Mom always praised me and believed in me, and I aimed to please her. She was so amazed that I would bring these delicious pastries home, and yet I never once took part in enjoying them (in front of them).

What I never told my mom is that when I would pick up the pastries before I delivered the papers that day, I bought two sacks and put one in each saddlebag.

During my paper route, I ate one sack--easily done by a 13-year-old--and by the time I got home with the other sack I had no more appetite. I just never bothered to share that with my mother.

I remember the story told by my mother about coming out on the porch of the house on 21st in Lincoln and calling for me to come to dinner. I was probably about five or six then. I didn't answer, and she kept calling. Finally, the neighbor called across to her and said, "If you look under the porch just to your right, you will see him." Do all boys like to hide?

I was brought up in a Bible teaching church that I still appreciate and I absolutely loved God and the Bible. God gave me a passion to know what truth is, and ever since a boy I just had to make sure I knew the Word of God. I read the Bible daily and pondered God's truth.

One evening after a meal, my mom was talking to me about spiritual things, which we did often after everyone else left the table. We talked about things like heaven and what is right and wrong. Mostly, though, we talked about Jesus.

That night my mother asked me, "Jerry, is there any reason that you have not been baptized?" I was thirteen and knew about baptism, and had seen others be baptized, but had not done it yet. I said, "No reason." So off we went to the church building that night and I was water baptized. The scripture calls it "buried and raised with Jesus".

So Phyllis, my mother, speaks today.

My mother always reminded me to teach Jesus and not elevate the church. The church is precious as the Body of Christ, all of those that come to Jesus are precious, but it is Jesus that we preach and worship.

When Mom graduated, all heaven rejoiced. My family and I were sorrowful and missed her deeply, but heaven rejoiced to see her home and at rest. As for me, despite the fact she wasn't physically here, it was as if she had never gone. Her spirit lives on in me to this day. Who she was and the inspiration she provided to me will never disappear.

However, her passing was very hard for my beloved sister Rona who was only ten years old at that time, along with brother Rod who was about sixteen. God bless Rona and Rod who continue to live incredible lives of courage, and Mom will rejoice to see us all in heaven.

Thanking God Always

Thank you, God, for these two beautiful daughters, Cherri Kay and Wendy Lynn. Thank for the wonderful joy they have brought to me and Donna. Thank you for Donna Kay, a mother to be honored indeed. Thank you for Your continued help to us through our life together.

Thank you God for my mother, Phyllis Ilene Esau Swanson. She was as precious as any mother could have been. She loved you, Lord, and she loved all of us. She loved my beloved Donna Kay and highly approved of her. I am glad they got to spend time together, and I believe they are both as angels on earth for me.

Thank you for my beloved Donna Kay who has always stood by me through all times–good times and hard times–always. Amen.

4. Christian friends helped (Kentucky)

"Then those who feared the Lord spoke with each other, and the Lord listened to what they said. In His presence, a scroll of remembrance was written to record the names of those who feared Him and loved to think about Him. They will be my people says the Lord Almighty". Malachi 3:16

God helps in Kentucky as we learn hospitality

Kentucky was sweet fellowship - The church family

IBM offered me a new job in Lexington, Kentucky, and Donna Kay and I moved with our daughters Cherri and Wendy. We quickly found a church and met many new friends who are still friends today. God helped us, but so did other people, especially His people.

Christians became like family wherever we moved, because Christians are supposed to be like Christ, and Christ Jesus is full of love and concern and truthful living.

Two of our good Christian friends were Jesse and Jane Gough, and since we lived so far from Kansas and Nebraska, the Goughs invited us home to the Jane's family, the Duvalls, for major holidays. Their hospitality was exceptional. They made us feel a part of their family right from the start.

One time while at the Duvalls, Jesse and I went hunting for arrowheads down by the creek bank in an "old holler". We built boxes to sift the dirt and find treasures. We heard thunder in the distance as we worked, and when we finally headed back to the house, it was a Kentucky downpour. Soaked to the skin, we laughed at each other.

Jesse often took me to visit with him at the VA hospital in Lexington. One of the men told me an interesting story—imaginary. The veteran told me that He and Jesus had started a new restaurant near Cincinnati. He said, "You know if you go to Cincinnati and a little north you will go right on into heaven."

Other wonderful Christian friends were Ken and Lee Baxter. They were gentle, loving people who treated us royally. One day when Donna and I said we were going camping, Ken and Lee told us to stop at Lees' brother and his family on the way down, which we did.

Then we went on to our campsite and were setting up camp in the dark, when Ken's family arrived with dinner prepared. The fried sweet corn was the best I'd ever eaten. What hospitality!

Kentucky is a beautiful place with lots of trees and "hollars" and interesting places to walk in the woods. The summers are very humid, so people just wait until evening to go outside when it is cooler. These pleasant visits gave us the opportunity to meet our neighbors.

Neighbors and friends are all blessings from God.

Condy and Nancy Cook were good friends from church and they suggested that all we go camping together. So Donna and I went camping with the Cooks, the Goughs, and the Baxters. We camped at Bee Rock.

We sat around the campfire singing hymns, while all around us, the evening sounds reflected back off the trees: katydids and locusts made music in the still night air. Despite the humidity, we had a wonderful time.

We were blessed with yet more precious neighbors, Stan and Goldie Allen. They came from eastern Kentucky and they were very good people and genuine. They would die for a friend, but a foe he would fight.

One day Stan invited me over to look at his TV (black and white), and he told me it was broken and we could have it. I took it home and was able to fix the TV. Then I invited Stan over and showed him that it worked. I then said, "Stan, I would like to pay you something for it." Stan looked at me and said, "I gave that to you, buddy!" I learned respect in that moment, and that to steal another's blessing was one of the highest forms of disrespect.

One day, Stan and Goldie's son, little Stanley, decided to mow the law. He tried one of the old used lawnmowers his father kept in a shed, but couldn't get it to start. So he went on to another, and another. After a while, little Stanley went into the house, and soon returned with his father in tow.

Then he and his dad disappeared in the pickup truck, and came back an hour or so later with a new riding lawnmower. Stan and his son took the mower off the truck and got it going. Off went little Stanley from house to house cutting a streak on his new lawnmower. "Watch out" Donna said to me as he came toward our yard. I rolled up the hose that was strung across our yard before he came in his tractor.

Friends and church family and friends have always been a blessing to Donna and me, and we cherish the relationships with many to this day.

Kentucky living - Family is the priority

Donna made do with her little house in the cul-de-sac in Kentucky. The lot was large, with an open back yard and room for a garden that we quickly tried to cultivate. The only problem was the the soil was clay and difficult to work. Needless to say, it was a challenge.

God helped us as we worked. We put some time and energy into it, and were soon able to plant seeds, which quickly flourished. One thing is for sure in Kentucky:

we had plenty of rain, sunshine, and humidity which made our garden grow green and lush.

Looking back on those days, with my job at IBM and Donna Kay at home with the girls, I realized that it is easy for a man to take new responsibilities in his job, be focused on it, and neglect his family. Donna Kay says I did not neglect her, but my word to younger husbands is to realize your highest priority is always God and your wife and your children then your job--in that order.

My good friend Condy challenged me, "Jerry, you will do more through your own children than through your own merits." In other words,

Make sure you do not neglect your family–keep them as a priority.

Cherri, me, Wendy, and Donna in Kentucky

Donna's family had kin in Kentucky and came to visit us. One day Donna's folks wanted to go see some Smith kin in Eastern Kentucky, and so Donna and I and the girls went along. We came to a town called Sligo about lunchtime, and there was a little diner dug into the hillside.

Eastern Kentucky is a place where people are generally poor. Anyway, we were hungry, and it was dinnertime. It was cozy place, and when we sat down, the waitress came. I asked if they had hotdogs for Cherri and Wendy. She said, "Pork steak, or ham." Then she called to the kitchen and corrected herself, "It's ham today."

When the waitress brought the food it was Kentucky-style: ham, potato salad, macaroni salad, coleslaw, and biscuits with coffee, and after all that food, they served us pie. When Grandpa Smith got ready to pay the bill, it was $1 per person. Not bad eat'n.

Grandpa and Grandma Smith (Park and Hollis) told a story of how they came to Kentucky on their honeymoon to meet kin in the late 1920s. Now Grandpa Park was a wise and careful man. As they were going through the countryside, they came on a creek. In those days many creeks had no bridge. You just drove across to the other side.

However, Park, being a careful man, got out and fetched a long pole from the hillside and stuck it into the water. The stick disappeared. He said it must have been about 12 feet deep. Just about then, he looked up and saw the ferryboat coming across the creek.

God is always watching over his people.

Cherri and Wendy started school in Kentucky, and by the time our family moved two years later they were sounding like southern gals. Real cute southern gals, of course.

I also want to mention nuts.

Grandpa Smith was sitting on the porch in Lexington cracking hickory nuts. About the same the time, I tried to shuck walnuts and got walnut oil on my hands. It went right through the gloves–I had dark oily hands for weeks to come.

Donna loves to crack the beautiful nuts at Christmas that you purchase at the store, but cracking nuts from scratch like hickory and walnut can be a real pain, and sure does make you appreciate being able to buy a nice package of nuts from the store.

Just another thing to thank God for, nuts, and all kinds of them ☺.

During the time at the Southside church, Jim and Mary Rackley and their children were missionaries to Africa. They shared their stories with us. Later in our life story, our adult children would go to Africa, but the Rackleys were our first exposure to Africa.

When my boss's boss interviewed me at IBM after we had been in Lexington two years. He asked me, "Where would you like to move next?" Those were the days when IBM meant "I've been moved." I said, "Well, I always thought I would like to live in Seattle."

Nothing more was said.

A couple weeks later my boss, Charley Moore, called me in and said. "I need you to go to Seattle." I said, "Okay". My job then was to go out to locations when someone had a problem with equipment that needed fixing. So I just thought it was another assignment. But Charley just sat there and stared at me. I said, "What do you mean?" Charley said, "I want you to go check out a new job." So Donna and I, with our pretty little girls, were going to move again, and to a very beautiful place.

5. Ebenezer - God is our helper (Seattle)

"Samuel named it Ebenezer, the stone of help. For he said, up to this point the Lord has helped us." 1 Samuel 7:12

Moving to Seattle was a blessing of God that Donna and I had never sought, but God just blessed us as a surprise. When we arrived in Seattle, two things happened as we went up the elevator in the hotel.

First, the elevator stopped midway between floors and opened to a concrete wall. Donna got the giggles at our predicament. We were blessed to be able to have a house-hunting trip on IBM and we had a good time.

Secondly, the thought came to me from that great song, "O thou Fount of every blessing ... here I raise mine Ebenezer... hither by Thy help I have come." God was faithful to us and we were thankful.

Donna and I have a plaque in our home to this day of Ebenezer, "The Lord is our Helper". On the reverse of that plaque, we recorded many events of God helping us. There are so many times He helped us, thus this book.

I realized a crystal-clear message from God again that He was with us, and had helped us thus far and would help us in the future, and to be at peace with God's plans–for they were for our good. So I pray for you.

God flooded our lives with precious people to help us beginning with Al Kelley, the IBM Area Manager, who connected us with a good realtor who helped us buy our first house in Highwoodlands area in Kirkland. That would have been about right around 1970.

Donna's parents had given us a gift that year of $1,000 that provided us the down payment for the $30,000 home. God helped us.

Our new neighborhood was full of tall fir trees and rhododendrons and azaleas, giving a fragrance that was grand. It was like living in a park all the time. Of course, if you know about Seattle, you know they get a lot of rain, and it keeps things very green.

We found a great church in Bellevue and fondly remember wonderful members of that church: Prentice and Barbara Meador, George and Maxine Mortensen, Bill and Vonda Fletcher, the Washburns, the Foxes, the Hackneys, Harvey and Jane Miller, the Petricks, the Parentes, the McClendons, the Bannisters, Jack and Ruthie Jewett (who we keep in close touch with still), Mike and Judy McClures, Gary and Marilyn Moungers, Eric and Faye Morris, and Larry and Carolyn Foster. I am sure we missed some names but all are special to us.

Cherri, Shelley, me, Jennifer, Wendy

Not long after we settled in Seattle, we were asked to take in foster daughters Jennifer and Shelley West. So, for a season, we had four daughters, and when we went to parent conferences, one of the teachers asked, “Now is this daughter yours?” and so on. We had one girl in Kindergarten, one in first grade, one in second, and one in third.

We have been blessed to have Jennifer and Shelley in our lives, and Cherri and Wendy were good big sisters to them. We still care about them very much, and now they have families of their own. God bless us all indeed.

Going to those school conferences helped me learn about myself. As the teacher said good things about all of my daughters, I felt a certain amount of pride that I’d had a part in that good outcome. And when the teacher expressed a concern, I realized that those issues were also reflection of me, and made me want to be a better parent and bless my beautiful girls.

We had good times with the Gene and June Bannister family. They lived in the country, and one day, while we had been invited over for a meal, they showed us around their property. As we toured the bunny cages, Gene said one of his small guests who had visited recently had picked up what he thought were raisins at the rabbit cages and popped it into his mouth. He chewed a bit then spit it out. “Yuck, them ain’t raisins.”

When you don't grow up around the farm, you want to be careful what you put in your mouth.

During this time, the woman who I called my second mother, Laura Lee, died. After my own mother passed away, my dad married Laura and they helped manage the children's home at Culbertson. They adopted Dona Rae and Deanna Esau. Laura had several children of her own, but the only ones we still know are Eddie and Dee Lee in Kearney Nebraska. Eddie has been a preacher all his life, and has been a blessing to many.

This was another hard time for both Rod and Rona, my younger brother and sister, but they went on with their lives. Rod joined the navy and Rona married and ended up in California. Rod decided to live in California, too, after he left the Navy.

Laura Lee fought a valiant battle with cancer just five years after marrying my father. Because of work commitments, I wasn't able to go to her funeral in Kearney where they lived at that time. Later Dad married a wonderful lady also named Donna Pearl Johnson Hinton. She was previously married to a Hinton and her husband had died from cancer.

Ray and Donna came to visit us in Seattle, and we took our two daughters, Cherri and Wendy, for an adventure. We rode the ferry to Vancouver Island and saw Buchart Gardens, which we all agreed was very beautiful. We also camped out in the Canadian campgrounds. I was impressed with the piles of free firewood at campsites. We had a wonderful time. We got to know the new Donna (our new mom) very much. She was a doll just like my own Donna Kay.

It was a long way for anyone to come to visit in Seattle. Jerry and Judy Selby came to visit along with their beautiful daughters, Lisa, Julie, and Connie. Jerry had served in the Navy out of Seattle and he called it "The moldy corner of USA." Moldy is right. Most all of the roofs are covered with shake shingles, and plenty of green moss covered them.

We were also blessed by the Ken and Lee Baxter family who came all the way from Kentucky to visit us in Seattle. After a day visit, one of the daughters said, "Let's go the beach." They had brought their swimming suits. Oops. They did not know that the Washington beaches are cold, and are full of driftwood that is brought onto shore by winter storms.

God bless our beloved daughters Wendy Lynn and Cherri Kay who grew up to be such beautiful ladies. They are always a joy to us, and we thank God who watched over them and kept them safe. We are so thankful for good friends who had a good influence on them along the way.

Jerry loves his daughters Wendy and Cherri

We miss the berries and fruit

It was also a fruitful life as we learned about the fruit available over the mountains in the late summer: pears, peaches, apples and, best of all, bing cherries. We drove over in our Volvo station wagon and came back loaded down with boxes of fruit. We ate the bing cherries all the way home–just like bears.

A great place to buy fresh fish was the Pike Place Market, and Ivars' Fish and Chips down town on the pier of Puget Sound couldn't be beat for atmosphere and delicious food. Yum! Puget Sound was absolutely beautiful when the sun would shine. I remember the first time I noticed that on a sunny day it was like no one came to work. People were taking off to enjoy the weather. If you go to visit, try either July or August and probably September to catch some sun.

While living in Highwoodlands, we enjoyed a cozy home with a free- standing wood fireplace. I often went with a group of neighborhood men to cut alder wood for fire. One of the neighbor couples went to cut their wood and while the wife went home to prepare the meal, the husband cut down a tree and it hit him and killed him. We were so sad for them, and I was always more careful when I went for wood.

Cherri was a great help to her mom. She has always been an organizer and encourager. She is upbeat and fun. She encouraged her sister Wendy and their friends to put on plays and games for the neighborhood.

Wendy was a wonderful daughter and had a way of saying things that allowed the truth to come through. One day she said to me, "I think we have a problem in our house."

I thought for a moment but didn't know what she was referring to. "How's that?" I said.

"We don't do what we say."

I knew exactly what she meant. I'd said I would take up the rug in her bedroom to let the hardwood floor show. But I had procrastinated doing it.

I got her tactful message, and got the job done right away.

Serena and Kyle are born.

As Cherri turned about nine or ten she started a campaign to add to the family, and so after some discussion, Donna and I agreed.

About nine months later our family was blessed with a beautiful daughter, Serena Dawn. When I arrived home after work one Friday, Donna said, "It's time to go", and it was. Serena was born at Evergreen hospital. Her name means "peaceful" and her middle name, Dawn, means "beautiful break of day." Serena was always a cherished treasure and a wonderful addition to our family. She has grown up to be a beautiful and talented lady, wife, and mother.

Then just two years later, God blessed us again with our son, Kyle Ray. It was my heart's desire to have a son, but I always said I would be happy with another daughter. Ours were so special. When they made the announcement at church that Donna and I had a new boy, you could hear the church cheer.

Kyle and Serena with their dad

Kyle's name means "integrity" and "from the strait", implying resources of God's plenty like mountain fjords. He has lived up to that name as you will see further in the book. His middle name, Ray, means "wise counselor". Kyle rode on my back in a carrier wherever I went around home or on an outing. He and Serena grew up being on the go, just like Cherri and Wendy, living life fully.

Soon after Kyle was born, a couple of things happened: first the Hackneys (friends and Realtor for Donna and I) found a larger house for us and we moved so that we had room to grow. It was a lovely house and we thank the Lord for being so good to us.

The other thing I learned was that Donna's job was tougher than my own.

I learn about the vital role of mother

Soon after the birth of Kyle, Donna had surgery on her legs and she needed rest to heal. I took off time to take care of Serena and Kyle and serve my beloved Donna as she recovered. I remember being proud of my ability to handle all the daily chores and let Donna rest.

However, one day as I had prepared a casserole and was taking it to the table, I dropped it–but I calmly cleaned it up and recovered. Then as I was carrying Kyle on my back, we bumped a potted plant off the stair ledge and down it went onto the light colored carpet on the stairway. I calmly got the vacuum and cleaned up the mess.

Finally, the third accident happened as Donna lay on the couch in the living room, and I was taking Kyle off my back in the carrier. My watch caught and the band broke. I took the watch, and out of frustration, threw it against the wall and Donna just laughed.

I looked at her and said, "What do you do?"

She said, "I cry."

"How often?"

"About once a week."

My eyes were opened to the life of a homemaker.

God helped me with a blessed and faithful wife in Donna Kay. Salute to Moms!

God blessed with special friends

After our move to the nice new house, we did not have sufficient or nice enough furniture for the living room. Friends from church had a party and brought us a cherry tree and encouraged all to put money on the tree. Our dear friends, Jack and Ruthie Jewett, gave us a beautiful handmade couch of maple and beautiful cloth covering. We were blessed.

Singing at weddings

Donna and I were part of a singing group for weddings. One song that I sang to Donna was "You fill up my senses", by John Denver. It was a favorite at wedding receptions. We also sang many other love songs including "Sunrise, sunset, where have the years gone?"

Thank you John Parente for allowing us to participate in the weddings.

Road to better marriages

Life goes by so quickly, and trying to keep a family "on course" while having job responsibilities, pressures, and church responsibilities is very difficult at times.

There were several couples from church, including Donna and me, that would have a marriage retreat each year in the mountains. Donna and I served as the cooks. There were two couples that liked to talk about having a good marriage. One of them invited us to a special retreat that changed our lives. We will share that later in this book.

The Lord helps us learn as we go

By God's grace, children become teenagers. We recognized early our need for God's for wisdom and understanding. God's grace was clearly poured out on us during these years. I was only thirty-four years old when we had teenagers.

We had not received any training in child rearing, and as we raised up our family, it was difficult in two ways: just physically being able to provide all that was needed, and then the wisdom and patience and insights needed to help your teenagers grow.

We have compassion on families trying to make it in this culture-- especially those with several children. However, God is able and will help.

Once again, God helped us, and much of that help came through the church friends, that is, the body or family in Christ Jesus--people who genuinely cared about us.

We had one car during those days--our faithful Volvo station wagon. Donna kept the car so she could take the kids where they needed to go, and I rode the bus to work, leaving at 6:30 a.m. and coming home at 6:30 p.m. Meanwhile Cherri and Wendy rode the bus to school. Sometimes Donna took them, but usually they opted for the bus. I think maybe they were embarrassed with our old car.

At times, we needed help with the car situation. If the car broke down or if we were going in different directions, our wonderful Christian neighbors, Norm and Kathy Graumann offered one of their cars. They were wonderful godly neighbors and Christians. God helped us in many ways.

Camping Fun with Great Friends

We had some fun times together as a family while in Seattle. Eric and Faye Morris went camping with us at Ohanapecosh in Rainier National Park. We had great time camping and talking. Eric and Faye were joyful people to be around, and all our kids grew up quite hardy from learning to "rough it" camping.

Jack and Ruthie had a cabin near Mount Rainer, and our family visited them at the cabin. We had lots of good times of games, food, and fellowship, then tucking in bed with a cozy sleeping bag. Their children were Scott, Leslie, and Matthew. They were like family to us, and still are.

One time Jack and I ventured out and rented an RV, and we did a joint vacation to the Pacific Ocean near the Olympic peninsula. What a fun time we had, all ten of us sleeping in that RV. Kyle was a youngster and he slept in the bathtub. What good memories.

We took a long hike on Cape Alava which went out three miles to the ocean through swampy area on a boardwalk, then a trek down the ocean coast about three miles (the tide had to be out), and then back about three miles on board walk. I carried Serena on my back and Cherri carried Kyle on her back. God helped us. God bless Cherri.

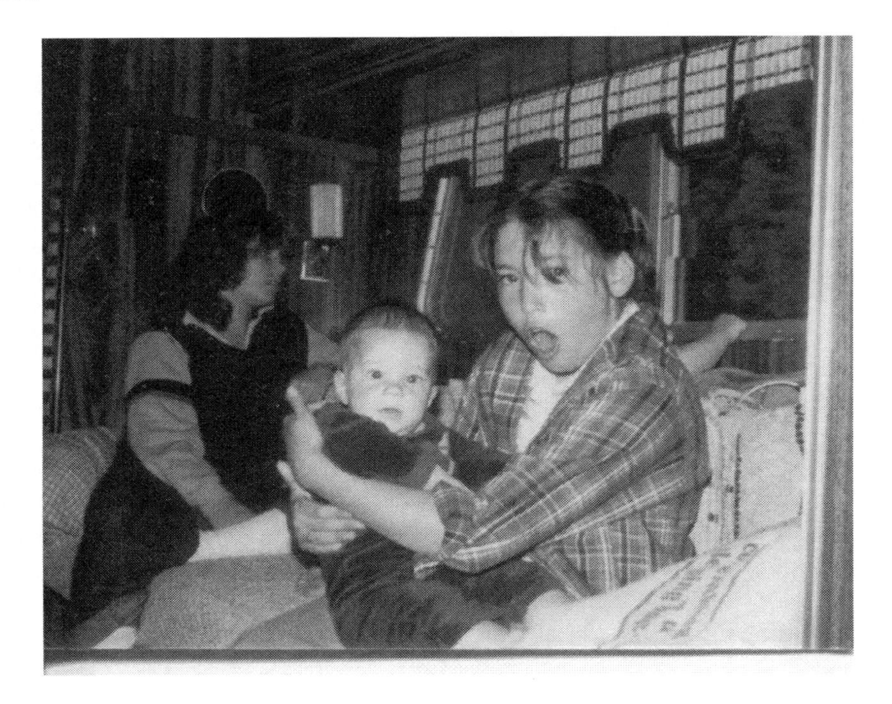

From left Wendy Lynn with Leslie Jewett holding Kyle in the RV we rented

I love Donna and our children

I went on a management-training trip to New York, and while I was gone, on the weekend I called home to see how the family was doing.

One of our teenage daughters answered,

"Okay Dad. What do you want?"

"Are you okay?"

"Yes dad, oh no, Kyle is choking" Clunk!"

I tried calling back for a couple hours but got no answer. We didn't have cell phones then to call or text.

Finally, after a few hours, I tried again and our daughter answered the phone. "Yes Dad. What do you want?"

"Are you okay? Where have you been?" I was thinking they were probably at the hospital or doctor or whatever,

“We went shopping. Why?”

"Is Kyle okay?”

“Yes.”

God bless teenagers and God bless the teenagers’ parents.

The family decided to go back to see the Swanson kin in Nebraska, and since it is a three-day trip by car from Seattle, we took the train. We got a sleeper for the nighttime. It was a real adventure. On the train, you do not get assigned seating and so we were fortunate to get several seats adjacent for all six of us.

We did have a good visit in Nebraska to see my folks and a good trip home.

God always helped us through our troubles even though we seemed to have more than our fair share, but as the scriptures says :

> *“The righteous face many troubles, but the Lord rescues them from each and every one”. Psalms 34:19*

Trying to be a good dad

I realized that I was not as patient as I should be as a parent, but I tried. Jack Jewett gave me a book, “How to Really Love Your Teenager” which suggested the wisdom of looking for any open opportunity to connect with teens since they resist being with parents, in general.

The concept of unconditional love grew in my heart over time.

I remember trying to get our family together for times of devotion to God and I felt that I was probably, at best, a C student as a parent.

One particular time I managed to gather our family together and asked them all to join in scripture and prayer. One daughter seemed totally disinterested in this attempt to do these devotions at home. So I said something to her, like do you want to leave?

She said, “Can I go now?”

“Yes“I said.

As all the family left the scene, I sat there, feeling pretty sorry for myself. As a father, I wanted to make a difference, but I obviously wasn’t doing a good job.

Then it dawned on me. That is just how God feels. We are often too busy and disinterested in His wanting time with us. Thank you Lord.

During those teen years, there was a group that came to the home church in Bellevue and they helped with outreach and training for youth. It was a time when a light bulb came on for our beloved daughters, Cherri and Wendy. We were so grateful for that moment. We are also thankful to Larry Foster who was a precious influence on our girls as preacher.

Both Jack and Ruthie Jewett, along with Mike and Judy McClure, worked with the youth and were very helpful in showing love and understanding to Cherri and Wendy. It made a big difference in their lives. May God bless them for the time they invested in our family.

Sometimes some of the church couples gathered for fellowship at church. One Sunday, we decided to spend the afternoon resting at church. When folks came back that evening, they were all talking about what had happened that day. That was the day that Mount St. Helens blew. It was quite the event with ashes going all across the country. Later that year, we went to get Bing cherries on the eastern side near Walla Walla and the ashes were still on the cherries.

During those years, it dawned on me that I needed to give more attention to my family, and not quite so much to my job as manager of IBM and as deacon at our church. So I decided, after much thought, to resign as deacon at church. I thought maybe everyone would object since I was involved in many activities. The elders said, “Yes, and God bless.”

It was hard to balance responsibilities. One day on my rounds as manager at IBM, I was going to meet Jim Andrews on Whidbey Island for lunch. I arrived a little early and took a tablet and starting writing out all my burdens. It filled the page. I took a deep breath and prayed.

Then I turned the page over and began to write all the things that I could thank God for; it filled the page. To this day, I try to take time each day to thank God for all He has done for us and, upon doing that, the day’s burdens get lighter.

It was during this time that Cherri and Wendy did not like the school they were in as it had many bad influences and so we checked out Kings High School–a wonderful private Christian school. However, the $500 a month tuition was a lot of money then. So we prayed and went on by faith and entered them in the school. When the money came due, I received another job at IBM that gave me $500 a month raise.

God is so faithful.

This stage of life was hard and at times overwhelming, but God helped us. God worked many miracles in our lives, and we continue to see them through the next seasons of our life.

Thanking God Always

Blessed Lord of all grace and love, thank You for your bountiful blessings and giving us a fruitful life; four beautiful children, each a treasure from You. Thank You for wonderful Christian friends and neighbors. Thanks for Your marvelous creation of fruit, berries, fish, oceans, and mountains, and for the most precious gift of Your presence. Blessed be Your name, Oh Lord. I truly have ten thousand reasons to praise You. In Jesus. Amen.

6. Why Go on Living? (Seattle)

"Happy are those that fear the Lord all who follow His ways. How happy you will be! How rich your life!. Your wife will be like a fruitful vine, flourishing within your home. And look at all those children! There they sit around your table as vigorous and healthy as young olive trees. That is the Lord's reward for those that fear Him. May the continually bless you from Zion". Psalms 128

"How can you tell if a man is spiritual?"

Coach Mac (Bill McCartney) had won the national championship at Colorado University and had become a national leader of men through the Promise Keepers. Many looked up to him and saluted him for his courageous leadership.

One day, a pastor came to his church and asked the question, "How can you tell if a man is spiritual?" Then the pastor answered, "You can tell by looking at the countenance of his wife."

Coach Mac said that the words struck him to his heart. He looked over to his wife, and she did not look happy and blessed. Rather she looked tired and worn down. It stirred him to think about his priorities, and as a result, Coach Mac stepped down from this career, and he began to focus on his precious wife and home.

God will help us, as he helped Coach Mac, when we simply ask for help. Beware of neglecting your wife.

It is a tragic scenario in our culture that thousands upon thousands will spend their money and time and attention so they can win "the big one", yet very few will take time to give any honor to one who is a godly man and cares for his wife.

Our American culture totally bombards us with their definition of success. Men and women live their lives chasing after status; power; importance; their expertise as golfers, swimmers, bikers, marksmen, fishermen, business entrepreneurs, or many other things.

In the process of pursuit of success, God gets pushed aside. Marriage gets pushed aside. Dysfunction in lives creates the storylines for TV programs and movies. We worship drama and violence, and we compromise and become very calloused to sin and corruption. It is the way of life in the world. Faithfulness to God and marriage fade.

We were blessed to be invited to attend a marriage weekend retreat across the Cascades from Seattle. We enjoyed the time away and we also enjoyed the little times of sharing, the technique called "10 and 10".

This "10 and 10" technique was about writing on your tablet HDYF (How do you feel) about any subject. Then after writing 10 minutes, you trade notebooks and read the other's note, and with a heart set on understanding and love, you would work to understand your mate with attentiveness, compassion, and understanding. It was good for us.

On that Sunday morning after some time together in the main group, we were assigned a "40 and 40". We went to our rooms and wrote on "Why do you want to go on living?"

Wow, I thought, could you actually ask such a direct question?

In writing that morning, it became crystal-clear to me that my reason to go on living was to raise a Christian family. A family that knew God's love, that was loved by me and Donna. A family that could grow and become all God had in mind for them. God has answered that dream over the years–fifty years. Praise God.

The primary foundation for a Christian family is that the father becomes a man of God and leads his family. We feel very blessed. Our children turned out great in spite of our mistakes. God helped us.

We are still working to be the example of a godly marriage and godly parents and godly grandparents. We continue to pray blessing over our family each day and seek the wisdom of God.

Vision of a godly Christian marriage and family

Yes, we go on living each day. Lead us one day at a time sweet Jesus. Here we raise our Ebenezer. The Lord is our Help. We have no other Rock but our God. There is no short cut to a successful marriage. You live life one step at a time. You keep praying and bowing your knee and lifting your voice to praise God for the victories. We have done that now for over fifty years of marriage, and it just gets better and better. Trust God and spend time with Him in authentic and humble prayer, and then rise up and live your life in confidence that God is able to do all things. Amen.

The vision of a Christian family has been a focus on the important priorities of our life, our marriage, and our children. Thank you, Jesus, for helping us up the road. We have been so blessed to see our feeble efforts and sustained faith bear good fruit by the mercies of God. Thank you Lord for being the God, and the God of second and third chances. Thank you for not giving up on me. Amen.

7. Beautiful children, blessed of God (Indiana)

"When I think of the wisdom and scope of God's Plan I fall to my knees and pray to the Father, The Creator of everything in heaven and earth. I pray that from His glorious, unlimited resources He will give you mighty inner strength through His Holy Spirit.

And I pray that Christ will be more and more at home in your hearts as you trust in Him, May your roots go down deep into the soil of God's marvelous love.

And may you have the power to understand, as all God's people should, how wide, how long, how high, and how deep His love really is. May you experience the love of Christ, though it is so great you will never fully understand it. Then you may be filled with the fullness of life and power that comes from God.

Now glory be to God! By His mighty power at work within us, He is able to accomplish infinitely more than we would ever dare to ask or hope. May He be given glory in the church and in Christ Jesus forever and ever through endless ages. Amen."

Ephesians 3:14-21

While our family was still living in Seattle, I knew that IBM was closing down the Northwest region office. I was asked to take a job in San Francisco. I said, "No, but I know about the Indiana office. Please see if that will work out."

It did work out. They said there was an opening in Greencastle, Indiana with IBM location. But both Cherri and Wendy were in a Christian high school now, and this would not be an easy move for them.

I prayed and then asked Cherri to come and talk, and I was sure she would not be happy with the move. It would be hard to leave her friends at that stage of high school. So, as we sat the kitchen table to have a talk, Cherri opened up the conversation and said,

"What's this about, Dad? Are we moving? Where to?"

Her questions indicated an openness to the fact that we needed to move. Thank you God for helping us throughout our lives. You even moved the hearts our children, even in difficult decisions.

We did move. We moved to a beautiful home in the country south of Greencastle, Indiana, an answer to my heart's desire to always live in the country. Donna was okay with the place, although, like so many houses there were pluses and minuses.

Before we bought the house, I had visited Greencastle without Donna, and looked at a few homes available then, and made an offer on the house that was accepted and that we bought. Then I went home for Christmas to get the family and move after the holidays.

When we arrived at the home in Indiana, the neighbor, Bob, came over to see me. He seemed quite concerned. I had asked for a survey of the property to be done on the three acre little ranch, and the surveyor discovered that the actual property line ran through a beautiful horse barn that the neighbor had built not realizing the boundaries were not aligned. The neighbor was in shock. What would he do?

He apologized to me and had no idea what would happen. Meanwhile the Realtor working for me said, "You should make money on this." When I understood the problem, I simply said, "Bob, why don't you go down and have it recorded as it and I will sign the paper and meanwhile we can be good friends." And we were.

But far more important than fences were our beautiful daughters and my beloved wife and Serena and Kyle growing every day.

It was big shock for Cherri and Wendy to move from Seattle, a large city, with everything you need and a lot you don't, to the little town of Greencastle where there was one movie theatre, and to go the bathroom during a movie you had to go across the street to the public facilities.

Beautiful Wendy Lynn Swanson
High School

Meanwhile I started my new job, and Donna began fixing up a home with her normal special touch. Donna worked on the garden while Cherri and Wendy went to South Putnam High School and Serena and Kyle went to Reelsville Elementary, in Reelsville, Indiana.

Cherri and Wendy both made many friends. They were involved at school and Wendy played basketball and she was pretty good. They found two dogs—both Labs, one black, the other a golden.

We are so grateful that both Cherri and Wendy chose to serve the Lord and walk in His ways. They have always been beautiful to us and before the Lord, and later God gave them wonderful husbands and families.

Beautiful Cherri Kay Swanson – High School

Southern Indiana is a beautiful place with warm summers where the grass grows so fast that we bought an old riding lawn mower and had to cut the grass about every four to six days. One of God's wonderful creations–the lightning bugs–were prolific on summer nights. One night they were so thick the air was electric. It was so amazing it seemed unreal.

Our special friends Jack and Ruthie Jewett came to visit with Scott, Leslie, and Matthew. One of the fun events was a hike in the Southern Indiana woods with streams and waterfalls. While taking a break, Cherri and Leslie let out a scream. The tall tree they were leaning on had a long black snake resting next to them.

One of the people I worked with at IBM was Ron Fite. We got together with his wife, Shirley, and sons Ron and Randy. They had moved from California to Indiana and that was quite a change for them also. They became friends and began going to the Cloverdale Church with our family. God was looking over us.

Our house was next to the state penitentiary property and, on occasion, either the cows or a prisoner got out. One day I made a call home in the afternoon to talk to Donna to see how things were going and someone answered with a gruff voice, "What do you want?"

I said, "I want to speak to my wife."

He said "She is okay, don't worry."

I hung up the phone and my mind began racing a hundred miles an hour. I checked out of work and drove home as fast as I could down that country road south of town.

I got home and everything was fine, everyone okay. I must have mistakenly dialed the prison. Whew. God helped us.

Jerry and Donna Kay in Indiana

My job took me to Florida for a project over the New Year holiday. After it was finished, I took the family down to Florida and we enjoyed Disneyworld in Orlando. Kyle was about three years old as I slid down behind him on the dark mountain ride. I told him to keep saying the verse Psalms 27:1 "The Lord is my strength; of whom shall I be afraid?" Kyle enjoyed the ride just fine. Others--even adults--refused the scary ride.

Praise God for helping and watching over my family while I was away for a season with IBM project.

We needed a new car and we bought a new Pontiac with a diesel engine. It turned out to be a good car. One of things I had warned our daughters was to be careful driving on gravel country roads since she had not experienced that in Indiana.

She said, "I know, Dad, don't worry."

Shortly after that, she came around the corner with a frightened look and said they had an accident on the road. She looked okay, but they had little Kyle with them. He was probably about four at the time.

I said, "Is he okay, and are you both okay?"

"Yes."

"Then the rest can be dealt with."

The front end of our new car was totally smashed, but I'd made my point: People are far more important than things.

There was a precious girl named Patty that we picked up on the way to church. She enjoyed the sweet fellowship and our daughters, Cherri and Wendy.

One night, on the way home from church in the dark country road, Donna said, "There is something in the road. I see the green eyes."

As I "pulled back the reins" on the Pontiac, it appeared--a huge black bull right in the middle of the road. Thank you Jesus for keeping us safe again.

God expands our family

One night the phone rang and the pastor at the Cloverdale church asked me if our family could take in three children who needed a home. He asked us to pray about it and call him back. So we did, and we called him back in about thirty minutes and said, "Yes, we can help."

He said, "Fine, we will be right over."

Whoa! I was not ready for that.

So here they came that evening. There were three precious ones named Renny (11), Alex (3), and Candy (5). All their clothes were in black plastic bags since they were homeless. The dad mentioned that they had lice in their hair. Anyway, they became part of our family.

We loved and took good care of the Lett children and prayed with them and took them to church and treated them well. Our Serena and Kyle were kind to them and patient to share. Donna had a lot of work to do getting them all ready for school and preparing meals and laundry, and all the other household tasks that having extra people in the house entails.

Kyle, Serena with Renny, Candy, and Alex

One of the favorite songs to sing on the way to church was "Shut de door, keep out the devil, shut de door from the devil in the night, shut de door,keep out the devil, smite the devil and everything will be all right." They were taught about Jesus.

Meanwhile, Cherri and Wendy were beautiful young ladies growing up, and we prayed for them every day.

Wendy remembers the time that a family showed up at church going from Florida to some place out West and they were desperate for help. They had little toddlers and had been sleeping in the rain and they were just needing a lot of things. I invited those people home. Wendy remembers saying, "Oh no, here goes Dad again".

It turned out for the good, as we were able to help that family. Donna washed diapers and fed the family, and I helped the dad with his truck and things they needed. We gave them some money and blessed them on their way. Wendy shares that she remembers that experience to this day as one that opened her heart to compassion.

We pray for Renny, Candy, and Alex to this day and hope that they will find God in their life and let Him work His plan for good.

Meanwhile our beautiful daughters, Cherri and Wendy were approaching the age of heading for college.

You can count on me, Dad - Cherri goes to College

I was not prepared for what lay head. College years came so fast. Here was my first beloved daughter, and she was ready for college, and life was just spinning with so many things. Raising a family is just not easy at all, especially a big family.

I remembered a wise man from our Denver days, and I sent him a letter looking for advice on what to do about college. The man sent a letter back and said, "Surely you have made good investments and are prepared for such." Oops! I was looking for some compassion and encouragement.

One day as I was pondering the situation (Cherri wanted to attend Abilene Christian in Texas and I was hoping she would consider York as it would be affordable), Cherri came in the door and said, "Dad, I've decided that I will go to York." Thank you Jesus for directing the heart of Cherri.

After arrangements were made, I loaded the Pontiac with all the things Cherri wanted to take. When I was done, there was barely room for me, Cherri and Wendy. We left after work on a Friday night and drove all night to York, Nebraska from Greencastle, Indiana. Donna Kay stayed behind with Kyle, Serena, Renny, Alex, and Candy.

When we arrived the next morning, we dropped off Cherri at the dorm and thought maybe we could visit some with her before going back home. Cherri came down stairs from her room and said, "Dad, thanks, I am all right, you can go now".

My eyes watered as we left our cherished daughter at college. Wendy and I got in the car and drove back home to Indiana.

Sometime later, a letter arrived from Cherri stating, "You can count on me, Dad. I will be a warrior for Jesus. I am okay, do not worry about me."

We never worried about her at all, but kept praying. She made up her mind to serve the Lord and it is the greatest thing to happen to a parent.

The summer after her first year, Cherri went to live with Kim and David Gustafson in Hutchinson, Kansas (Donna's niece). Kim and David were a great blessing to Cherri. We are eternally grateful for the love and support they gave our daughter over that summer.

The next year, Cherri called us to come to York to meet Richard Houle. Donna and I arrived one evening, probably Friday. Donna went with Cherri to her room and I went to meet Richard. Richard was a Resident Assistant, and he said, "Wait here in my room while I deal with some things, I will be back."

I waited and waited, and about 2 a.m. Richard was able to get back to his room. He apologized for keeping me, then said, "I want to ask you if I can marry your daughter." I prayed with Richard, and then got some rest. The next morning, we gave them our blessings. Richard was truly the right man for Cherri and has been a godly husband.

During that year, Cherri invited us back to York again, this time to receive "Parents of the year at York College." Thank you Cherri for whatever you did to make that happen. We were honored because you chose to live honorably. All glory goes to God.

Cherri marries Richard Houle

Richard and Cherri are wed in York, glory be to God

Cherri and Richard were married May 10, 1986. It was a beautiful wedding. Serena and Kyle were in the wedding party. Cherri was beautiful and Richard was handsome. They made a positive impact at York College, and we believed God would be with them in their future.

After the wedding, they headed to Colorado to settle. We sure were proud of them. God took care of them. Later, they went to Oklahoma Christian College where Richard finished his degree and Cherri worked for Clinique while he went to school.

Meanwhile, when Wendy graduated from high school, she also decided to attend York College. She met Rich's friend Jack English, and Jack came to visit us in Indiana to approach us about our prized daughter Wendy. We easily accepted Jack.

Wendy and Jack were in a traveling singing group and we were so proud of them. In their last year at York, Donna and I went back for the performance of the year. Jack was the organizer, and he and Wendy sang a duet at opposite ends of the stage singing, “Somewhere out there, love will find its way.” Wendy sounded just like Amy Grant, and Jack sounded just like Michael W. Smith.

Thanking God Always

Lord God, Heavenly Father and Shepherd of our souls, thank You for watching over our treasured daughters Cherri and Wendy.

Thank You for choosing and preparing godly men, our son-in-laws for them, Richard Houle and Jack English.

Thank You for York College and all the dedicated staff that sacrificed to make a way for so many to obtain a quality education.

Thank You for providing Kim and David Gustafson who reached out to Cherri. Thank You, Lord, for my beloved wife, Donna Kay, who is always standing with me.

Lord God, Heavenly Father, bless our marriages, and also those going to be married. May we seek You all the time and Your ways for our lives.

In Jesus name, Amen.

8. Confirming God's path for us (Indiana)

"Who among you is wise and understands God's ways? Live a life of steady goodness so that only good deeds will pour forth and if you don't brag about the good you do, they you will truly be wise!

But if you are bitterly jealous and there is selfish ambition in your hearts, don't brag about being wise. This is the worst kind of lie. For jealousy and selfishness are not God's kind of wisdom. Such things are earthly, unspiritual, and motivated by the devil. For wherever there is jealousy and selfish ambition, there you will find disorder and every kind of evil.

But the wisdom that comes from heaven is first of all pure. It is also peace loving, gentle at all times, and willing to yield to others. It is full of mercy and good deeds. It shows no partiality and is always sincere. And those who are peacemakers will plant seeds of peace and reap a harvest of goodness."

James 3:13-18

God helps as we let Jesus be our life

Now that's my God

During those four years in Indiana, God moved us to a new place spiritually. We cherish the good years as the Lord guided us into more of His will.

While living in Indiana, a Christian neighbor, Bob, took me to a weekly Christian men's group at the Double Decker restaurant. The preacher of the church where we attended then said, "You should not be associated with others like that. We do not accept those outside of our church." I hated that attitude and prayed and prayed for God's wisdom.

One day on the way to work, God reminded me of the scripture in Luke 18 about two men praying. One was beating his chest and asking God to forgive him, a sinner. The other was looking down on that man in self- righteous pride and thanking God that he was a much better person than this sinner.

God said He rejected the one in pride. On that day, God set me free forever of judging the spiritual standing of others, and reminded me to mind my own path. Minding my own walk is lifetime job.

I kept praying and reading and re-reading scripture until late into the morning searching for answers. God showed me scriptures like "Christ in you is the hope of Glory "Colossians 1:27 and "If a person wants to boast, they should only boast of what the Lord has done." 2 Corinthians 10:9.

My life verse became Jeremiah 9:23,24.

"This is what the Lord says, Let not the wise man gloat of his wisdom, or the mighty man boast in his might, or the rich man in his riches. Let them boast in this alone: that they truly know me and understand that I am the Lord who is just and righteous, whose love is unfailing, and that delight in these things, I the Lord, have spoken!" Jeremiah 9:23,24

We settled in a church in Cloverdale where Curtis McClane was the preacher. Preacher Curtis was very learned in scripture, and taught with great wisdom and compassion. I could share thoughts with Pastor Curtis and have a good conversation with respect and compassion.

The Parkers and Witkanacks had backyard cookouts with a big bonfire and hot dogs. They were terrific. The Nicholson family and Sutherlands were treasured friends. God bless them all.

I continued to go with Bob to the Christian men's group at Double Decker. One day I gave the devotion and then I sat down. Albert Avery, who was sitting across from me, told me the story about when he was in WWI and their plane had become lost in the clouds approaching the mountain pass. As they circled, he could hear the wings of the plane hitting the tips of the trees.

Albert said, "I prayed, 'God, You have always said that You will help us in times of trouble and we are in trouble.'" Just then, he looked up to the front of the cockpit and could see the clouds part. The plane flew in that direction, and flew up and over the mountain pass. He said, "Now that's my God!!" as tears rolled down his cheeks.

I had been around a lot of religious people, but Albert was a man of simple faith. Albert, in one moment, warmed my heart with the essence of Jesus, growing and increasing my faith in an awesome God.

At another meeting, Albert looked at me and said, "Jerry, you are going to be a Gideon. Bring your checkbook and come to prayer time on Saturday." I did, and I became a Gideon on June 26, 1986 in Green Castle, Indiana.

Gideons are simply Christian businessmen from various churches who volunteer their time and treasures to place the precious, living Word of God in approved areas - what we call the traffic lanes of life.

One of the clear truths from God for me during this time was that the New Testament clearly states that we are now under the dispensation of the Holy Spirit. I read the scripture and accepted the promises of God. God promises us not a spirit of fear, but of power, love, and wisdom (2 Timothy 1:7). Not only did I believe the scriptures, I was hungry to grow in the freedom found in Christ and His Holy Spirit.

In Christ, we have One Body and the attachment is by, in, and through Jesus. We pray that all will seek the true path of God in Jesus and read His Word and follow it. Yet, God forbid that in following the right path for us, that we should degrade our fellow brothers and sisters. We exalt Jesus, not our church.

"We do not want your churches because they will teach us to quarrel about God."

Chief Joseph of Native American wisdom.

God forbid that we be known for our quarreling as Christians.

May God help us to remember our center and purpose is Christ in us, and may we be at peace with others in respect and honor, even if we do not agree.

We must follow our convictions, but also allow our brother to follow his convictions. The scripture that says "work out your salvation with fear and trembling ", 2 Timothy 2:12. The text continues "for it is God's spirit that is working in us". That is God's Spirit is working in each of us as individuals and, as for me, I remain the one (in Luke 18) asking for the mercy of God. God please keep my heart humble and forbid that I be the one looking down on others in self righteousness.

A foundational conclusion for me was that each Christian should do what they believe God wants them to do and to be. At the same time, each Christian should honor his brother and sister in letting them do the same. In healthy relationships we can talk with honor to each other.

While visiting Arlington Cemetery in Washington D.C., I read an epitaph on a grave stone of a Navy Admiral that settled with me, "unique as the waves, yet one as the sea".

God helped us again, even through times of spiritual growth in Him. We are all unique members of Jesus. Our blessing comes in Jesus, not what church we belong to. We lift up Jesus, not ourselves.

Jesus is our salvation, Jesus is our Hope, Jesus is our Anchor, Jesus is our Good Shepherd, Jesus is the truth, Jesus is the Way, Jesus is our Counselor, Jesus is our Master, Jesus is our Friend, Jesus is the Light, Jesus our Bread of Life, Jesus is the Living Water, Jesus is our High Priest, Jesus is our Friend, Jesus is the Lamb, Jesus is the Son of God, Jesus is Yeshua, The Messiah, the Holy Prophet, Jesus is Vine and we are the branches, Jesus is King of Kings and Lord of Lords, Jesus is the Word, Jesus is our example, Jesus is our Savior and Redeemer, Jesus is our Mighty Warrior, Jesus is our Judge, Jesus is our Advocate, Jesus is our Freedom, Jesus is our Alpha and Omega—the Beginning and the End and A to Z.

We have had known many wonderful pastors/preachers, teachers and elders over the years ;

Roger Hauley who was at York and who ministered to mom.

Wesley Filmon who was the preacher in Grand Island, Nebr.

Preacher Curtis McClane in Cloverdale, Indiana.

Larry Foster who loved as Jesus in Bellevue, Washington.

Les Pearson showed us the love of Jesus while we were in Rochester Minnesota along with his precious wife Roz.

Kent Hummel has been our wonderful and faithful pastor here in Loveland at Good Shepherd Church.

Our own Jack English, son - in - law along with daughter Wendy who serve so compassionately at Vineyard Church. Their love and example of Jesus will change lives forever.

My beloved friend, Pastor Phil Brewster who is a true friend, who listens taking time to share and care. He is a true warrior of Christ, leading others to reach the homeless, those in prison, and those who are broken to be healed in Jesus. Thank you Phil for being example of Jesus.

Jonathan Wiggins of Resurrection Fellowship combines love for the Word and welcoming of the Holy Spirit.

Carl Sutter with wife Vicki has been a fresh inspiration to me and to Donna Kay. His combination of humility and courage in a transparent and genuine walk are a great encouragement to all.

Greg Deal, Pastor of the Cowboy Church in Loveland is on the same page with me, calling men to be MOG .. men of God. I appreciate this blessed brother who has two jobs. You inspire me Greg.

Beloved Dennis Carlin who ministers as Pastor to Nation to Nation Lakota people in Pine Ridge. Dennis came to the Lord at the time of reading a Gideon placed Bible in motel and after seeking God became a missionary Pastor to the Lakota and has served 14 years laying down his life for the people in a very hard place. We pray for him and all the missionaries and Pastors that live Jesus in hard places and hard times.

Other Preachers/Pastors and Elders who I highly esteem include Prentice Meador, Larry Brewster, Doug Kehr, Jim Barrington, Scott Cox, Mike Denny, Eddie Lee, Elliott Osowitt, Fred Evenson, Tom Albracht, Rick Olmsted, Blake Bush, Johnnie Square, Bill Anderson, Gary Glover, Brian Thompson, Larry Kidwell, Jim Rice, Dave Gustafson, Steve Sears, Fred Urben, Jim Lewis, Dennis Merk, Larry Brewster, David Goltz, Laurence Hinton, Bert Morrison, Phil Wilgers, Bill Riley.

Surely the reward is great for those who serve faithfully whether a leader or follower of Jesus. Jesus said "even a cup of cold water given to another will not go unnoticed" Matthew 10:42.

Of course the best sermons come from those who humbly walk with Jesus in the doing .. loving the sick, the homeless, those in prison, the widows and orphans

... that is where Jesus reigns. And then there are the mothers who lovingly minister to their children day in and day out.

My salute to all who preach the Word of God with both the love of God and the fear of God, and who are approachable in Jesus. My special salute to those who let Jesus keep changing them day by day and live with a humble and transparent example of action to others.

Thanking God and praising Him

Thank you, precious God and Jesus and Holy Spirit. Truly Your Spirit is such a blessing to us and our lives. We receive all that you have for us more and more. Not to our glory. Not to our credit. We praise Jesus. He is able to help and heal. He is mighty to save. We stand and proclaim that He can be trusted to do anything at any time. Hallelujah God. We believe. In Jesus name, Amen.

9. Warm times in a cold place (Minnesota)

"Have you not known? Have you not heard? The everlasting God, The Lord, The Creator of the ends of the earth, neither faints or grows weary. His understanding is unsearchable. He gives power to the weak, and to those who have no might He increases strength. Even the youths shall faint and be weary, and the young men shall utterly fall.

But those that wait on the Lord shall renew their strength; they shall mount up with wings like eagles, they shall run and not be weary, they shall walk and not faint" Isaiah 40:28-31

God was good, as He always is, but it seems that in Minnesota we were able to see Him more at work in our lives. I don't know if it's because we sought Him harder there, or because life was a little less hectic, or what. He was not only working His plans in us, but we could see that He was active in our lives.

When we moved to Minnesota, Serena and Kyle were growing up, demonstrating their talents and their maturity as they tried to prove to us that they could be responsible. When the Swanson family moved to Minnesota, the Lett children, Renny, Candy and Alex, went back to live with their father. We were sad to see them go, but we knew it was time. For them, and for us.

Cherri was married now to Richard and they were living in Rifle, Colorado. Wendy was still at York College with Jack.

What sweet times we had in Minnesota as a family . God was always looking after us. Nothing that we did deserved His kindness. He is a merciful and loving Father. We praise His name.

Donna always said Jerry was hopelessly romantic

God ended up blessing us with a wonderful home in the country where we had land, trees, a stream, and a river nearby. The seasons were marvelous–long days in the summer and beautiful white winters. In the winter, we took advantage of getting out and playing in the snow.

IBM was in Rochester, but we lived in the town of Kasson near Mantorville, Minnesota about 15 miles west of Rochester.

Donna began fixing up the country home, Serena and Kyle started to school, and I got busy at IBM. Our good friends from Indiana, Ron and Shirley Fite, with their sons Randy and Ronny also moved to Minnesota and they remained good friends.

Wendy marries Jack English

Meanwhile God blessed us with a major event.

Jack and Wendy, a beautiful couple,
at their beautiful wedding.

Jack and Wendy got married on May 22, 1987. It was a glorious wedding in Grand Junction, Jack's home town. Wendy was absolutely beautiful and Jack was handsome. They went on to Oklahoma Christian College and both graduated with degrees. We are so proud of them.

Wedding party for Jack and Wendy

During the early years of marriage for both Rich and Cherri, and Jack and Wendy, they came to Minnesota to visit for the Christmas break. We had really good times.

God helped us find a church family and got involved. In the process, we made friends with Sandra who is now married to Bob and we keep in touch. We also are friends with Louise Meyer who lives in Duluth, and we cherish friendship with Julie and Steve Suprenant who we have a close relationship with since they come and see us in Colorado from time to time. Steve has also gone to Promise Keepers with me.

God blessed us with wonderful Christian friends and neighbors.

Fun family times in Minnesota

Those were very fun times of playing games inside, playing in the snow outside, and eating good home cooking including plenty of festive foods. Sometimes the cold winds of Minnesota would drive the temperature down with wind chills in the range of 70 and 80 below. At those times, ice formed on the inside of the walls and windows. Thankfully we had a workhorse of an oil furnace that worked overtime and kept us warm. We also had a fireplace and lots of firewood. Kyle loved to split wood and build fires.

During Christmas break, Jack and Wendy and Cherri and Rich would come home to Minnesota for a good visit. One of Jack's ideas was to let each person decide what we would do during the Christmas break. The list would go up on the refrigerator, and we worked down the list. It ended up that after college Jack and Wendy came to live with us for a while and we truly enjoyed their company.

Serena on Colorado Lady with Nugget tagging along.

Jack found out that Serena wanted a horse so he helped get her one. Of course, few things in life are that simple. Along with the horse came the need for fencing and a shed. Jack helped me get all that done. In the process of building the shed into a hillside, we used picks to move the wall of dirt, where we found old artifacts such as bottles and buttons. We hadn't realized until then that our place was located where the old stagecoach stopped.

Serena was a good rider and she did not put up with any nonsense from Colorado Lady. I was a novice and learned quickly from her. The barn that Jack and I built down on the bottom of a hill along the stream that ran all winter long was very cozy. Donna, Serena, or myself would go down each day, and give the horse some oats and brush her a little to keep her used to being handled. Donna was the most faithful in chores.

We moved to a new church near us, Salem Road Church. We are still friends with Pastor Les Pearson with wife Roz. We cherish all our friends there, including Dave and Linda Mosbo who took us north to fish and enjoy the wonderful loons, and the Edmondson and Isaacs families. We also remember well the Byers family, Dr.

Dave Warner family, and Ron and Sheryl Peterson, the Huebners, the Capps, the Danielsons, the Lewises, and the Hokansons.

Kyle to hospital

One night when I came home from work, Kyle was on the couch sick. Donna said, "I think he has the flu." Somehow, God prompted me to go into my cove office under the stairs and take down the health book and open it. It fell open to appendicitis and I said, "I am going to call urgent care." Urgent care confirmed the symptoms after I did some poking, and they said to bring him in.

It was an icy cold night and it would be hard to get in to Rochester from the country; we were about 15 miles out. Our car was a big Chevrolet with rear wheel traction, so I loaded some sand bags in the back and let some air out of tires for better traction and took Kyle in. Urgent care sent us to the hospital and when he was in his room, he had a lot of visitors–young doctors who were doing their residency. Each one came in and did their "thing" including poking his abdomen and asking, "Does this hurt?" After the third time, I said, "The next person that pokes Kyle will get poked by me." Suddenly, there was no need to hurt my son any further.

Kyle and Serena participated in the Bible Bowls at church. It was a family event on weekends. Steve and Linda Lewis helped spearhead those events. We had lots of fun.

Praise God, as Kyle had the operation and was healed to be a healthy lad.

Both Kyle and Serena were baptized in those days. They were growing in the Lord. I am so proud of how they both grew up to serve the Lord with all their hearts.

Kyle in Minnesota

Kyle was learning to play the trombone at school, and he also was quite involved in science fairs that the school hosted. Kyle also became a good woodsman, cutting and splitting wood, which came in handy since we had the fireplace and often needed to supplement the oil furnace when temperatures dropped for days on end.

Mentored in the Gideon ministry

It was during this time that we got very involved with the Gideon ministry. They made me camp president, and we were encouraged to set some high goals. In this, we saw another way that God helped us. There is no way we could humanly accomplish these goals.

We hosted the state convention. I worked with the hotel manager who was not a Christian. I invited him to come and bring his girlfriend to the pastor's banquet on Friday night.

At the banquet, as the manager sat at the table with his girlfriend, with Donna and me, he asked about the goal of so much monies we had posted on the banquet banner.

He said, "Do you plan on raising that much money this weekend?" "Yes we do," I said.

Later that week when I went over to the see the manager, the first thing he asked was if we met that goal. "Yes we did, with God's help."

Gideons are sacrificial people. One of the members of our Camp was Dr. Morlock, Billy Graham's personal doctor. I asked him one time for any advice he wanted to give. Dr. Morlock said, "Always go in twos." I appreciated that good advice to this day.

A precious Gideon, Stan Attleson, was my humble mentor in the Rochester days. Without his love and guidance and fine example, I would have made a lot more mistakes, possibly losing the opportunities to influence others through my testimony of how God is working in my life.

Blessed with good friends

Ron and Shirley were good friends and a blessing to us. Ron had the gift of making us all laugh and also of providing leadership wherever he went. One day at work, I was called to the nurse's station. Ron was having a heart attack. The ambulance transported him to the hospital where he had emergency surgery.

Shirley was with him in ICU and I visited each day. I always carried my Bible with me, and we'd read scripture and pray together. One day the nurse said to Shirley, "Your pastor has been up to see him regularly." Shirley came into the room, and there I was. We both laughed about that when she told me what the nurse said.

Ron had worked hard to pursue nomination for his son Ronny to go to the Naval Academy. The acceptance ceremony took place before he got out of the hospital so I went on his behalf. I was also able to visit Ronny at the Academy on one of my IBM trips. It was an amazing place–especially the huge picture of "Duke", John Wayne, in the main building.

Later on, Jack and Wendy went back to Colorado to begin a business there, and Rich and Cherri came and lived with us for a while.

We had a lot of fun with them. Rich helped me build a wonderful barrier wall around the back of the yard. Both Jack and Richard were hard workers.

Winter fun

In the winter, we did our best to go cross-country skiing. We also liked sledding, so the fact we lived on top of a hill that became a great sled run to the bottom was a great asset. We had fun. Sometimes we went out at night and played in the snow at Christmas when Jack and Wendy and Richard and Cherri were there.

One night Jack brought home the movie "Rocky", which I had not seen. I really enjoyed the movie. After the movie, I was so motivated that I got dressed and went out in the cold winter night with snow and ran up and down the hill just like Rocky. They all thought I was crazy.

Winter is okay in Minnesota but you better have a garage for your car and a parka for your face and ears during January when it never gets above zero for weeks.

Serena, Wendy, Cherri, and Kyle on steps in Minnesota

God rescues Jerry

One day on the way to work in that red Chevy, I was heading past the little town of Byers and I saw a blue van approaching the highway crossing. I was sure it would stop, but it did not. In a split-second, I turned and went down into a ditch, going past a huge steel power pole, and then drove back up the other side onto a dirt path along a cornfield. I stopped and said a prayer of thanks that all was well and noticed in the rear view mirror that blue van was going on. I thought all was fine, because I had not felt any impact.

So, I drove on down the ridge of the cornfield and got back on the highway and began to go on my way to work. About that time, someone drove up beside me on the highway and motioned me over. It turned out that the man had captured the license of the van. I said, "That's fine. I don't think he hit me."

"Yes, he did."

So I looked to the back of the car and it was all caved in. Wow.

So, I thanked the man, and returned to the coffee shop in Byers and called the highway patrol who took the information and was later able to track down the van. While waiting for the highway patrol, I pulled out the little testament that I carried (a good habit for all Gideons so they can give them away as witness). The testament opened to this verse:

Psalms 91: 11 "He orders his angels to protect you wherever you go. They hold you with their hands to keep you from striking your foot".

Praise the Lord, what a promise, what an awesome God. God was telling me that He was watching over me and my family.

Men of God - Promise Keepers

Jack invited me to go back to Colorado one year for Promise Keepers. I did and took Kyle, and it was a wonderful experience of men coming together from all over the country to sing and praise God and hear excellent speakers. We ended up going every year and one year our group grew to more than twenty.

It was during Promise Keepers that we were released as men to lift our hands in praise to God--to show our joy and "break down the walls", to be men of openness to share and pray. It was a great time of transition for me and for Kyle, Rich, and Jack, to be with thousands of godly men who were seeking God. When our focus is Jesus, there is freedom.

Kyle and Rich went with me to the Washington, D.C. Promise Keepers event on October 4, 1997. It was a wonderful experience with over one million men all seeking to be men of God. Kyle and Rich are both mighty men of God and I love them with all my heart. I thank God for Jack who first got us started with Promise Keepers. This ministry has been such a great encouragement to men.

Steve and Julie

Two of the best friends of our life are Steve and Julie who grew in the Lord while we were at Rochester. They moved away and we moved away, but we have remained good friends ever since. They are a blessing to us.

Dear friends Steve and Julie during Minnesota days

Steve and Julie returned to Colorado for a week during our celebration of 50 years of marriage. They have been very dear friends and an inspiration to us of love and acceptance.

I have found very few people who have true friends that last. Cherish those that you have. Nourish and nurture those relationships, no matter how many miles and years separate you. Tell them how important they are to you. Lift them often to the Lord in prayer.

Enjoying Christmas, praising You, Jesus

Living in Minnesota was a wonderful time of growing in freedom in the Lord as Donna and I worshiped at Salem Road Church. It was so special to be free to worship the Lord with joy and peace. One of our favorite times of the year was Christmas.

Pastor Les and Roz invited our family over every Christmas Eve to enjoy focusing on Jesus and not so much on gifts. Of course, Christmas in Minnesota was truly white with snow and cold so we all bundled up with our parkas. Singing Christmas carols is one of our special joys. We love to praise Jesus! Below is a picture of our wonderful daughter Serena Dawn in Minnesota days.

Serena, beloved daughter during days in Minnesota

Beloved Serena and Kyle

What a blessing both Serena and Kyle have been to us. We had many good times in Minnesota living in the country and enjoying our wonderful church family at Salem Road. Kyle and Serena both have grown to be exceptional adults with their families. Surely God helped us.

Beloved wife Donna Kay, her parents graduate

I praise God for my beloved Donna Kay who has always been a great homemaker and true companion. She worked at home sewing, cleaning, and cooking, making our home a sanctuary. She was a huge support to the children in all of their activities, making certain the children had what they needed.

Donna has always stood with me in ministry, whether it was at church, with the Promise Keepers, or with the Gideons. She has always been good at taking care of our own children and enjoys working with the children at church. She is an incredible blessing to me as she is a good listener. She has been a frugal and wise wife. I am so extremely blessed to be married to her.

While living in Kasson-Rochester, Donna's mother, Hollis, became ill with stomach cancer and graduated to heaven. She had lived a good and an honorable life, passing into the arms of Jesus at the age of 81. Donna's father, Park, continued living on the farm, passing into glory a number of years later at the age of 91. Praise

God that the life of the godly goes on after they die. Their lives influence us, and certainly Park and Hollis live in our hearts to this day.

What a wonderful blessing for us to have godly parents, and Donna's parents were a great blessing to us. We traveled to Kansas each year to visit them, enjoying the farm and helping them in the field or garden. We played board games in the evenings, and always encouraged each other with our shared hope in Jesus Christ.

Bats are coming

One evening while the family was on the large deck overlooking the hills and trees and streams, Serena pointed and said, "Look, what is that?"

Bats were coming out of our chimney. She counted more than thirty of them.

One night as Serena and Kyle were watching TV, a bat came through a slit in the fireplace and started flying around the room. With the kids screaming and ducking and hiding, the whole event soon turned into a circus. I took some screens off the windows and gave one to each of the family to help guide the bat without hurting it. I opened the patio door to give it a large enough escape hatch if it wouldn't go out through a window, and finally it went out.

When another bat came in through the same way another night, I resolved to take a more proactive approach. When winter came, I plugged the hole. No more bats. However, we also missed them next summer since they had taken care of our mosquitoes.

Yes, we never forgot Colorado

Whenever we could swing it, we came back to Colorado for a vacation. We loved the mountains and all the fun associated with camping and hiking.

Still, our Minnesota days were precious. And while not everything was good or what we would have chosen for our lives, God helped us through it all. He is so good. We lived there about seven years. It was while we were in Minnesota that we celebrated our 25th anniversary.

Good news is ahead as God provides a way for us to return to Colorado, to call it home, to live near the mountains and our adult children who were now living there.

Kyle, Serena and Papa Jerry
on top of the Sand Dunes Southern Colorado

Thanking God and praising Him together

Well God, we just cannot say enough thanks for Your good news and kindness to us. You rescue us, You help us through hard times. You blessed us with wonderful sons-in-law. You took care of our parents. You placed us into good church families. You bring us into good Christian ministries and events that encourage us and help us grow. You are a great and awesome God. Meanwhile You cover our marriage and keep it strong. We love and appreciate You. We lift up Jesus and welcome the Holy Spirit. Praise be to Your name. In Jesus' name, Amen.

10. God grants the desires of our heart (Colorado)

"As the mountains surround Jerusalem, so the Lord surrounds His people from this time forth and forever" Psalms 125:2

Going back to Colorado was where our hearts were, but how did we get there?

One day I called Gary Goulet, my good friend, who then worked at IBM Boulder. "Hey, Gary can you get me a job back in Colorado?"

"Would you come here?" said Gary.

"In a heartbeat," I said.

Six months later, Donna and I were safe and sound–residents of Loveland, Colorado.

God is our helper, and thank you Gary.

When I made the initial trip to check out the job opportunity, I went to the Minneapolis airport. I decided to get a coffee after checking in at the gate I was departing from, but I had to hurry because when I came back, they were boarding the plane. So I got on, got comfortable, and off we went. I made some conversation with the man next to me and relaxed, anticipating my arrival in Denver.

As we got ready to land, the pilot announced, "Welcome to Cleveland."

I said to my fellow passenger, "We aren't in Cleveland,"

Imagine my surprise when he said, "Yes we are".

I went right to the woman at the gate and told her I made a mistake somehow and got on the wrong plane; I was going to Denver.

She said, "No problem, just go down to this other gate, and here is a pass for you."

While my recollection is a little hazy at this point, I am pretty sure it was Delta Airlines who helped met, but I was soon on my way to Denver. Thank you Delta, and thank You, Lord.

I now worried about being late for my job interview. Since this was long before cell phones and email, once I was settled on the plane, I picked up one of those phones in the back of the seat, ran my credit card, and made the call.

The secretary said, "Don't worry, Jerry, Rick decided to take the day off, see you tomorrow."

God is always helping. Praise His name. I got the job.

The actual move was all paid for by IBM, but we had two cars and two dogs. We decided to drive instead of fly so the dogs would be more comfortable. Donna and Serena drove in our Oldsmobile, while Kyle and I drove in the red Samurai jeep that we inherited from Rich and Cherri. The dogs, Tal and Nugget, rode with Kyle and me. Since the Jeep was a ragtop and no A/C, we drove with the windows down and dog hair flying around. It was interesting, noisy, and hot. Besides that, we topped out at 55 m.p.h.

Being back in Colorado was wonderful on several accounts. Rich and Cherri lived in Loveland, and Jack and Wendy lived in Ft Collins. We lived in Loveland, and it is a beautiful place to live. The first priority was getting up a dog run for the "boys" (the dogs), which we did quickly and it was mid-June.

During that summer, Donna and I took Serena and Kyle hiking every Saturday, and then on Sundays we went to the early service at church so we could get in another hike in the afternoon. We had wonderful times in the mountains. God's wonderful creation is seen in the Rockies, and I always feel closer to Him there.

Jerry and Donna, Jack and Wendy in back, Cherri and Rich and Kyle and Serena in front

God Places us in a Wonderful Church

As the fall came and went, and Christmas was near, I said to the family, "We need to find a church and settle down."

We had been visiting several churches trying to find the one we thought God wanted us to attend.

I invited Blake and Kristin Bush over from Good Shepherd Church. They were youth pastors, and I thought that would be a good opportunity for Kyle and Serena to meet them.

So our family actually drew names (cast lots) out of a hat to decide where they we would attend. The church selected was the one where Blake and Kristin were youth pastors. It is the same church Donna and I attend today, Good Shepherd Church, or as one of granddaughters used to call it Big Shepherd. Both are accurate names for Jesus.

I had my new job and Donna had the home and big yard to tend. Serena and Kyle had a new school to go to, and that was very hard. It is hard to leave your good friends and move hundreds of miles to a new place.

They were blessed by wonderful older brothers and sister though– Rich and Cherri and Jack and Wendy. They also were blessed by their small group leaders at church, Mike and Amy Nappa. Thank you to Nappas and Bushes for your kindness and service.

Again, God helps the family, but so does the church family.

Serena graduates

Serena graduated from Loveland High and went to school for a while at Christ for the Nations in Dallas. It was again a very hard transition for her with no friends, but her cousin Susan Swanson (now Susan Miller), became a precious friend and support to Serena. God bless you, Susan.

Serena came home and attended CSU for a season, but I was not able to keep her support going. It seems as though we have always struggled with finances, and every time we saw our way out of one situation, we landed in another. I didn't like that I was never quite able to properly provide for all the needs of my wonderful children, and often felt I was letting them down in one way or another.

I know Serena would have excelled at college had she had a chance to finish. She got a job at Home State Bank, and is excellent at whatever she does.

You will see later how God was so faithful to work out His plans for Serena even though her high school and college days were very difficult. Serena has been a servant to her parents and others around her.

Erica, Serena, Debbie and Clare–they came to visit and enjoyed Rocky Mountain Park and the mountains.

God Blesses our Family

Our family went to Ouray for a vacation. We took a jeep ride up on the backside of Mount Sneffels in Yankee Boy Basin. We decided to hike to the top of the pass. We made it up to Blue Lakes Pass with an elevation of 13,100 feet. Little Ryker, at just a few months old, was not happy riding on my back, but he made the trip.

Donna worked that summer to plant flowers and a garden in the back of our yard on Thames, and it was beautiful. We lived near a wonderful walking path and park. Kyle took Tal and Nugget for a long run each day on the raised road off Boyd Lake. The dogs loved it.

Promise Keepers

That summer, we guys all went to Promise Keepers. It was in Mile High Stadium and we stayed in a motel in Denver and walked all the way over to the stadium. I had made a yellow flag so their gang could see where we were going. One mistake--we did not do a head count before we started over the Colfax bridge, and we lost my good friend Steve from Minnesota. We did not realize it until we got back to the motel. Fortunately God watched over Steve and provided a ride back in the dark that night.

Promise Keepers was a great opportunity for men to grow as godly men. Steve took the challenge and has become a men's leader in his church. I have always loved men's groups and men's ministry.

Proverbs 27:17 actually says, "As iron sharpens iron, so a friend sharpens a friend"

One of the worst things for a man to do is to isolate himself in his brokenness, rather than build authentic relationships where we share and pray for each other. Thank you Coach Mac (McCartney) for all you did to help men in Promise Keepers.

Kyle graduates and ventures out

Meanwhile Kyle graduated from Loveland High School and after some talk with the Navy, he agreed to delayed enlistment as long as they promised him language training, which they did. Kyle ended up going to Great Lakes Training the next fall in Chicago. Donna and I went to his graduation on Christmas Eve and stayed over to be with Kyle. He was totally exhausted mentally, physically, and emotionally. We were so proud of him and his graduating.

Kyle went on to Monterey and received two years of training to be equipped in Mandarin. It was a beautiful place and I was able to go visit him while he was there. Richard and Cherri drove all the way back to see him graduate at Monterey. Richard was like a true brother to Kyle.

Salute to Kyle Swanson, a true warrior

While Kyle was in Monterey, some Seals talked Kyle into joining them on the run team, and so Kyle did a lot of running in Monterey and was able to participate with the Navy "sixpack" run competition. They won in their competition. Kyle still likes to run and climb mountains.

Kyle excelled in all he did as a highly responsible and intelligent son who persisted in learning and applying himself. It is such an honor to salute this soldier and to know that he makes a difference wherever he goes. Of course, we all make a difference as long as we trust in God each day and follow His path.

Kyle still serves as Chief Intelligence Officer in the Naval Reserves. May God protect him and all who serve and sacrifice for our safety. May God bless our country as we seem to be losing our Christian foundation to many who have rejected God. May God help us.

Beautiful grandkids growing up in Colorado

From left Hannah Faith, Caris Grace, Amber Brook, Ryker Timothy holding Bryce Kyle, and Bailey Joy is down in front and on the end is Benjamin Christian holding Glory Hope

Cherri and Rich were blessed with four wonderful children:

Benjamin Christian, Hannah Faith, Caris Grace, and Glory Hope.

Wendy and Jack were blessed with four wonderful children:

Ryker Timothy, Amber Brooke, Bailey Joy, and Bryce Kyle.

Of course we just are busting with pride over our grandchildren. The ones named above now are all adults, and we recently celebrated the wedding reception for Ben and his wife Raela. Praise God as they go back to Belize where they are directors at Laugh out Loud Children's home. God bless them indeed.

Cherri and Richard attend Resurrection Fellowship, and both very busy raising their family, working, and doing ministry. We are so proud of them.

Jack and Wendy both serve at the Vineyard Church in Windsor.
Jack is the Campus Pastor and Wendy is in charge of the Marriage and Family ministry. They make a big difference in the Kingdom of God.

Ben took golf lessons with Grandpa

We wish more could experience the beauty of the mountains in Colorado–the streams, flowers, fresh air, and cool summer nights. We especially enjoy the mountain rainstorms and the breeze that dries things out quickly, and that wonderful sun that shines almost every single day of the year. Thank You, Dear Lord.

During the years of the grandkids growing up, we went to Ouray for vacation with the entire family. We rented a log cabin home and the grandkids all liked swimming in the Ouray pool. We had many good times hiking, jeeping, and swimming in Ouray.

Vincent Lemke

It was a great privilege to know an amazing mother named Linda Lemke, a single mom who raised three wonderful young men through faith and grit. We salute her. We love her and pray for her and try to help when we can.

Vincent was one of her boys who I was able to be a friend to during his upbringing. His father had no interest, but I did and I am so proud of Vincent and how he has gone through many struggles of life and become a success in the Marines. He now is married to Melissa and has two beautiful daughters Emma and Madi.

When Vincent and I were buds during his youth, we participated in a go cart event and I think it was for Partners; an agency to connect mentors to young people. Anyway, Vincent and his friend were just young fun loving boys. However most all the other participants in the race had dads who were far more committed to win than the boys and took winning very serious.

So as the event went on I told Vince and his buddy. "Hey, just go have fun". They did, and they won. It was a sweet victory.

Vincent also has two amazing brothers. Daniel has become a leader against sex trafficking in America. He rode a bicycle around America, over 7000 miles in fifteen months by faith and determination and now he is helping build jobs for those coming out of this terrible night mare.

Jesaja is another brother who has excellence in school and now is at Colorado Mines and he is a leader in Navigators, a wonderful Christian ministry.

We salute these wonderful warriors for the Lord and we praise Linda the mother. God bless indeed.

Erin comes to live with us

Kyle met Erin Portal in Monterey and asked if she could come and live with us, which we gladly agreed to. We prayed for Erin and showed her the love of a father and mother. She had to make some difficult changes in her life, which she did, with the help of God.

Erin is now married to Christian, and they are both nurses and have four daughters that we also claim as grandchildren. They also are serving the Lord with all their heart.

We cherish Erin and Christian. They are dedicated to the Lord and their family, and they are living courageously and compassionately for Him.

A Mission Trip to the Ukraine

I was asked to go to the Ukraine with The Gideons International, and I was blessed to be part of a group that shared more than 110,000 scriptures, mostly with youth who had never had a copy of God's Holy Scripture and had never heard about our precious Jesus.

Youth receiving their first copy of God's living Word in Russian . they gladly received "Spaceba"

"Is Jerry sick?" asked Sergei, as we rode in the van to the next school. Sergei and I were communicating through our interpreter Shasha, who said, "No, he is praying",

Sergei didn't understand. "What is he praying?"

I said, "Tell him I am praying that all the seeds that have been sown in the hands of those children will be planted in their hearts and grow, and that the devil will not be able to snatch them away."

Shasha shared and then Sergei openly prayed fervently for the same concern.

Praise the Lord. *Slava Bogu*.

A Second Career

I had a great career with IBM. I worked for many different bosses my career, and each one was different and each one treated me differently. I worked hard for each of them. God blessed us through IBM.

Colossians 3:23 "Work hard and cheerfully at whatever you do, as though you were working for the Lord rather than for people. Remember that the Lord will give you an inheritance as your reward".

Finding my second career was a challenging process. I read and prayed and decided to pursue visiting forty people to get advice and input. The very first person I visited was Tim Galloway. Tim "graduated"-went home to be with the Lord–at a young age (52) with a marvelous reputation of helping everyone he could. He was one of my heroes.

After visiting these friends, I felt the Lord was giving me the direction I needed, and I ended up going into Real Estate. It was a wonderful experience for me, and I was blessed to work with Larry Kendall and The Group Real Estate. One of my partners, Kelli Couch, became an exceptional help in working with customers with me. She is a gem.

I spent about fourteen years in Real Estate, which is a demanding job. During that time, I was also very involved in Gideon leadership and it was a true stretch. Somehow, God provided for us, and we met many wonderful people.

For several years, we had a Christmas party at Sylvan Dale for all the customers. One year, one of the grandchildren asked one of our daughters, "When can we go to grandpa's ranch again?"

I was grateful to many who did business with me and made it a habit of praying for my customers and their welfare.

After retiring from Real Estate, Marc Dykstra offered me a part-time job being an ambassador for their company promoting their Enviropest business to the community. I have enjoyed my time working with our customers and the current manager, Kevin Lemasters, who is a wonderful Christian leader and boss.

The Golden Years as Grandpa and Grandma

The Lord has been good to us and we cherish the years of being able to love on our grandchildren and to pray for them and help them when we can. We are proud of each one.

From left :Bailey, Ryker in back, Bryce and Amber Brooke.

Ben and Hannah back and Glory and Caris front

11. God expands our family (Colorado)

"Your wife shall be like a fruitful vine inside your house; your children will be like olive shoots around your table" Psalms 128 : 3

God blesses the joining of beautiful couples

Isaac and Serena are joined together

Serena's relationship grew with Isaac. Isaac came to visit Donna and me and asked permission for Serena to marry him. He asked us to write out a note so he had it in writing.

One day, they took a hike up on Horsetooth Mountain and they came upon a quaint setting with a table and two chairs. Isaac said, "Let's sit down and rest,"

Of course Serena, being very polite, said, "No way. This is someone's special little setup. "

So, Isaac, being Isaac, just sat down. Then to Serena's surprise, out came their beloved friends Blake and Kristin who had carried all that up along with the meal that they served to them.

Then, when Isaac, in private, proposed to Serena, she naturally said, "I need to get my parents' permission."

Isaac pulled out the note of permission for parents. Isaac did his homework and was prepared.

Serena and Isaac's wedding was wonderful, thanks to Jean Maggard and Diana Bruns and many others at our home church, Good Shepherd. Serena was absolutely beautiful and Isaac was handsome. We also remember the Hunts who brought a special car for them to drive.

One fond memory of the wedding was when Pastor Blake began the ceremony by saying, "Isaac, how did you do this?"

The audience laughed knowing that Serena was a true jewel and Isaac was the guy of confidence, and he won the prize. They have been a wonderful couple and have a long life of joy ahead with the help of God.

Isaac learned the trade of HVAC with the help of a church friend. Isaac and Serena settled in church with Blake and Kristen at Third Day Victory Church and serve and minister there. Isaac has always been excellent with the youth, and is an excellent husband and dad.

"Love flashes like fire, the brightest kind of flame. Many waters cannot quench love; neither can rivers drown it. If a man tried to buy love with everything he owned, his offer would be utterly despised" Song of Solomon 8:6,7

Isaac and Serena were married on March 25, 2000 at Church of Good Shepherd

Henry Isaac was born to Isaac and Serena. He has grown up to be a wonderful lad and a blessing to all his family and friends. We cherish him, as we do all our grandchildren.

Isaac and Serena Tyrrell went with Henry to Rwanda to do mission work–what a sacrifice and a big deal getting ready and getting everything into place for the trip.

Isaac shares the story of riding to work in his truck when he heard a program through Focus on the Family about orphans, and it touched him so much he had to pull over. He and Serena prayed about it and told Pastor Blake Bush about their desire to go to the mission field, and immediately Pastor Blake says, "We just got an opening in Rwanda."

So, they began raising funds, which they did well– God helped them, of course.

Within a few months, they were off to Rwanda, and not to steal any of their incredible stories, it was a three-year assignment that they did very well and went through many trials and troubles, but God brought them through it all. It was so special to receive Serena's blog updates on the internet and hear how things were going.

Then after two and half years, Isaac and Serena with Henry returned to what Henry called E-America. It has been so good to have them back home. Serena has mixed feelings, missing the joy of serving on the mission field. Meanwhile they are making a huge difference in their church community and wherever they go.

Kyle and Margie are Joined Together

Meanwhile Kyle kept saying that he would not get married–just no woman that he would want. I told him that when he met 'Miss Right', he would be like a puppy with his tail between his legs. Well, praise God, Kyle met that very special person. Her name is Margie Sharpe and she is as precious as can be and a tremendous addition to the family.

Kyle met that beautiful lady, Margie, who stole his heart forever.

They married on May 22, 2010 in Loveland at our home church. It was a beautiful wedding with brown and yellow colors, and Jack English did a wonderful job of officiating.

When Margie's family came for the wedding, we bonded immediately. The Sharpe family jumped in and did a great job of organizing the food for the wedding day.

We also were blessed by the Tyrrell family who pitched in and did a great dinner at the park for all the families. Thank you Tom and Jana. Thank you also again to Good Shepherd Church that allowed us to use their facility to do the wedding.

As the wedding was wrapping up, and Kyle and Margie were running to the car and rice was flying, you could feel this cool breeze blow over all of us. Donna said, "That was God's endorsement of this great couple." Amen.

We love Margie totally and all of Margie's family–Phil and Marcie Sharpe and all the family. Margie is a wonderful wife of Kyle, and we pray for them every day.

Kyle and Margie now have a precious jewel, Ruby Annabelle, along with brother Luke. We are so proud of them. We pray God will continue to bless and protect this beautiful family as they serve the Lord and raise up these little ones.

As I write, Kyle has taken a new job back up north in Colorado and we are so happy to see them move closer to all of us. We enjoy them so much.

Luke Swanson (son of Kyle and Margie)

Beloved Ruby (daughter of Kyle and Margie)

Thanking God and Praising Him Together:

Thank you, Lord, for blessing our family. They are so precious to us. We thank You that you give us protection and provision. Thank You so much for allowing us to come back to Colorado. Thank You for each of our cherished treasured children who have all grow up loving You and serving You. Each of our children bless us more than we can bless them. You are an awesome God. Thank You, Jesus. Amen.

Off We Go to Africa

During the second year that Isaac and Serena were in Africa, they were not able to come home for Christmas, and Isaac's dad, Tom, said to Donna and me, "You both need to go to see Isaac and Serena and Henry in Rwanda. "

I said, "We do not have the money to do that."

Tom said, "Pray."

We prayed, and God provided and we were able to go to Rwanda for a month. It was one of the highlights of our lives. We thank Tom for the nudge, and for financial help from our home church via Robin Parker, and for help and good advice from our good friend Bill McIntyre.

Isaac and Serena were marvelous directors of the Home of Champions and impacted the lives of all the orphans and the mommas that helped. God used the talents of Isaac and Serena to encourage and shape with the more than sixty Champions who lived with them. I remember their happy voices early in the morning about six a.m. as the children headed out to school.

The simplicity of the life in Rwanda was wonderful–no distractions such as radio or TV, just the sounds of birds and the fresh smell of the earth and the local cooking fires.

Here we are in Rwanda Africa with Serena and Isaac

12. Glory be to God (Colorado)

" I look up to the mountains – does my help come from there ? My help comes from the Lord, who made the heavens and the earth. "' Psalms 121 :1

God's Glory in the High Country

Praising God and climbing mountains

One of our favorite activities is going to the mountains for a hike or a walk. I am always ready with a daypack, water with a filter, something good to eat, rain jackets, and a map for the trail. We have hiked all over Colorado and some of Wyoming. Great is our God!

There is never a day when we go to the mountains that I am not inspired by Almighty God's beauty in His creation. It's the peace and quiet and the calmness of the trees and birds and streams. Praise the Lord.

Jerry and Donna spent many good times on the trails and still hike. Just going a little slower

Pawnee Pass

Donna and I, along with Kyle and Serena, like this trail. It is out of the Indian Peaks area, and the hike starts out on the flat going past Long Lake. We always enjoy the flowers as we go up past a beautiful waterfall when the climb comes up onto a plateau, which you hike across until you come to the last mountainside climb which requires going across a snow field and up to the top level of the mountain.

If you walk to the edge, you're overlooking the other side of the mountain looking down on Lake Granby. It is steep down the other side on a goat-like trail. It is beautiful and well worth the hike.

At the top of Pawnee Pass, you're 12,500 feet up. It is cold and windy. Whenever you get up high, the weather is very cool or cold and windy. If you combine that with rain, sleet, or snow you are up against it. Be prepared.

Estes Cone

Donna and I, along with Kyle and Serena, Rich and Cherri climbed Little Estes Cone. It doesn't seem like much of a mountain, but it took some huffing to get to the top of the trail. Cherri brought M&M's, and it was a good source of energy as we made our way to the top. It turned out to be a great outing.

Chapin Pass

Donna and I were on our way to Grand Lake for our annual honeymoon, and we drove over Fall River Road on a mid-September day and took a hike up to Chapin Pass. As we arrived at the pass and looked down the mountain to the valley below, it began to snow. We huddled down in the rocks and then decided to head back. The snow was gentle and beautiful, almost mesmerizing. We had a good day because we were well-prepared. Praise God. We heard later that day that the snow kept coming and it caused the Forest Service to close the road for the winter. We were glad we left when we did.

Up Beaver Meadows

Donna and I with Kyle and Serena were hiking up the trail on a nice summer day and having a good time when we decided to take a rest on a couple logs. While resting, we kept smelling something really ripe, and as we got up to leave, we looked behind the log. There lay a dead elk that the coyotes had been working on at night. Whew.

Bridge of Heaven

One of the Ouray trips with Donna and me and Kyle and Serena included a Jeep drive up to the access point on Horse Thief Trail and then a hike up to Bridge of Heaven. It is a beautiful hike through a forest of aspens and the trail pops out on a ridge overlooking Ouray. We saw a huge Mountain Sheep ram on a ledge looking like he was guarding the area. We kept climbing a ridge until the trail turned along a sharp ridge which if you fell either way you would not stop for a long distance. We ate our lunch and, as typical in the high country, we saw a storm developing, but we chose to take a nap in the aspens on the way down.

Then the storm came and we put on our rain jackets and made our way off the mountain. The trail turned into a small stream, and our feet were soaked by the time we got back to camp. The rule in high country is "do your hiking early and be prepared to get below timberline (about 10,500) before the lightning comes".

Many are killed by lightning strikes in high country. God was watching over us. Thank you, God.

On the Bridge of Heaven hike with Donna and Wendy on another day, I tried to find a shortcut. After an hour or so, the shortcut through deep forest left us stranded on a cliff with no outlet. We had no choice but to turn around, press through the deep forest and underbrush again, and work our way to the main trail.

Life is like that so often. God gives us a clear path through the beautiful woods and we get bored or impatient and look for the shortcut only to find that we made a big mistake.

God says in Psalms 37,

" Be patient and stay on the path God has for you."

Lawn Lake

Kyle and I took a wonderful backpack trip into the backcountry. Since this hike is in the Rocky Mountain National Park region, we had to get a camping pass a week before. We loaded up our packs and hiked the six miles to the junction near the lake. We would have been happy--and thankful--to stop here, but our permitted overnight camping spot was up over a ridge to a beautiful high mountain meadow.

When we arrived, we set up our tent, It was about 4:00 p.m. and we were worn out so we took a nap. At about 7:00 p.m., we woke and Kyle said to me, "Let's climb that ridge up through the forested area." So, we took a light pack and started up through the forest to an area that looked intriguing. As we went up through the wood, I kept marking the trail. At sixteen, Kyle was annoyed with the delay.

At the edge of the woods, I stopped and tied my hanky onto a tree limb, and off we headed up the tundra until we finally arrived on top of a rock outcropping. As we stood on the top of the rock, it appeared the entire world lay before us. A herd of elk enjoyed a beautiful lake in the valley off to the north. To the west, we admired Longs Peak. At over 14,000 feet, we felt we could reach down and touch it off to the north.

Shortly after, we witnessed a most beautiful sunset going down behind the saddle off Mt. Fairchild. Then, as we turned and looked way down below at the tree line, it just all looked dark. Of course, our eyes adjusted some to darkness as the sun sank behind the horizon, but we were both glad I had marked the trees along the trail. Otherwise, we might have spent the night looking for our campsite.

The next day, we loaded up and went over to Lawn Lake to camp. We set up in our designated place and made sure the rangers could see our license attached to the tent, and about then the ranger did show up and told us to be careful. Apparently there had been a mountain lion around that area recently.

After camp was set up, we took off for a walk around the lake in our flip-flops, thinking we would just go for a short stroll.

A little walk turned in to further and further as a result of urging from Kyle until we actually reached the mountain saddle above, and Crystal Lake to the left. The mountain sheep moved off to the side of the clearing and blended into the rocks.

I remembered the Rangers words during the night, I heard what sounded like animals scampering. I realized what I'd heard was probably deer running from that mountain lion.

We saw plenty of deer in the camp area. It was a wonderful trip in a beautiful place. Going up and going down, the trail ran beside a creek coming off Lawn Lake. The area was beautiful, and we found many places to stop to cool down and get drink of cool water along the way.

Fern Lake - Jerry and Serena

Serena was a tough hiker and camper, and she did very well carrying her pack on a trip to Fern Lake, one of those places where the density of the forest made it pretty wet and the mosquitoes were terrible. Fortunately, Serena brought some repellant. She also brought a book to read and went to our tent to escape the thick droves of tiny pests. It was a lovely place and we crossed the Big Thompson River along the way. We had a great time and it was no problem going with Serena. Some hikers are lazy and some seem to travel with BA (bad attitude), but all of the Swanson kids were tough and did not complain.

I tried to pass on the importance of good shoes, moleskin insoles, and along the way to rest your feet and put on moleskin on as soon as a blister started to rub. If your feet are cared for, you can endure a lot.

Also, have lots of good water. Carry a water filter to allow you to fill your water jug as often as you like. In the Colorado mountains, it is normally dry, so you need to have lots of water in your system. You might think you are not sweating but you are, it is simply evaporating and the water is gone.

The other priority is to be prepared to keep warm. A rainstorm can come up in minutes and you need good rain gear to stay dry. As a worst case scenario, you can use a plastic poncho or black garbage bag. The best kind of clothing is wool. Dress in layers and definitely bring rain protection.

If you talk to my friend Steve, who got trapped overnight on a mountain, he always prepares for a possible overnight stay even when on a short day hike. Be ready to stay warm–carry matches and kindling to build a fire. Come prepared with a compass, a map, a flashlight, and something to carry water in.

Think ahead and be wise.

Winter hike

Hiking with Serena was a pleasure because she does not complain and she is organized, and so we decided to go on a winter hike in Rocky Mountain National Park. The wind blew, making the air really cold. The snow blew into our faces and all around, creating little whirlpools. Since there was snow on the ground, we wore snowshoes. We stopped along the trail at noon and fixed lunch with a small backpack stove. Pretty soon we had a pot of water boiling to make soup. It sure was tasty. There is something about being outdoors and being hungry.

As much as we enjoyed our day, it sure was good to get home again where it was warm.

Winter camp out

Kyle, being adventurous and young, wanted to go camping in the winter. We loaded up and when we got to Cameron Pass it was -3 and snowing. The group included Kyle, Jack, Richard, and me. Snow was piled high all around us when we loaded up our packs, put on our snowshoes, and took off down Michigan Ditch trail.

After a few miles, we decided to head down a slope into the snow and woods and try to set up camp. Richard worked at packing down a spot for our tent to go while Jack and Kyle worked at building the fire to hopefully warm us. Because of the cold temperatures, the deep snow, and the wet wood, it was really hard.

The winter days are short and we felt the oppressive cold which made us work slower than we wanted. Soon we realized that our trip was quickly turning into more of a survival trip than anything to do with pleasure. Keeping a fire going was very hard and keeping our water bottles from freezing was a huge challenge.

I remember how cold those boots were the next morning. Made you think maybe walking barefoot would we warmer, but we knew better. A moment of chill was worth it to keep our feet dry, which was actually more important than keeping them warm. We made some attempts at breakfast, but ended up packing up our stuff and loading up before we headed for the Explorer.

On the way, Jack asked for the keys. I tossed them to him. He said, "I'll get the car started and warmed up."

Thanks to Richard for picture of Jerry, Jack, and Kyle. We stopped on the porch of an old cabin. Unfortunately, we could not enter so we camped in the snow.

Uncompaghre

I wanted to climb a Fourteener, as mountains more than 14,000 feet in altitude are called, and I found a spectacular mountain on the map in the middle of the San Juans, up out of Lake City on the way to Engineer Pass and Ouray. What I liked about it is that it was only 3-4 miles to the top from the access point on jeep road. That sure sounded better than many of the six- to eight-mile approaches, which, when doubled, makes a long hike.

Our trip began. Rich, Kyle, and I headed down I-25 to Walsenburg, over Wolf Creek Pass, and down into Monte Vista. The sun was going down, so we took a gravel road south. At a dead end, we set up camp and spent the night. It rained.

The next morning dawned clear but cool, so we headed up through South Fork and over Slumgullion Pass and came to an overlook just before Lake City. There we laid the tent out in the morning sun to dry and we rested a while.

A couple men drove into the parking area, and I went over to the older bearded man and ask him about Uncompaghre Peak. I could see it sitting high across the mountains, and it appeared as if it would really be difficult to climb. The older man said, “No problem.”

Whew, that put me at ease-- sorta.

As we drove the Explorer up Nellie Creek later that day, we found a place to park. We didn’t have to carry our packs far to camp, and we were soon settled in for the night.

We would climb the peak the next morning.

It was a beautiful climb up the mountain, and the top was just spectacular looking up north to the Blue River and Cimarron River watersheds. I counted what seemed to be at least 100 peaks in the 360-degree view.

We took the trip on over Engineer Pass and into Ouray where we were able to shower and swim in the famous community hot springs pool. We had planned to stay the night, but after some dinner, we decided that with three drivers we might as well drive the eight hours home to our own beds, which we did.

Never Summer Wilderness

Rich and I had planned a trip with Kyle and Steve around Never Summer Wilderness one summer, but Rich had an accident and could not go. Steve came from Minnesota, and Kyle went with us, but we three were very sad to not have Richard along.

We started at the access of Long Draw and entered the Grand Ditch--the headwaters of the Colorado River. There was a large bull moose in the road who rambled off as we headed out for what was about a 25-mile trek. We talked about where we were going, and Kyle decided to go ahead and set up camp at the reserved site for the night.

After hiking most of the day, Steve and I turned off to Lake of the Clouds and our camping site. When we arrived, it was dark and wet with snow still on the ground. It was also raining.

But no Kyle.

Steve and I decided one of us should stay at the camp, Steve stayed, and I went back down the mountain where I met Kyle coming up the trail in the rainstorm. All turned out well.

The next day we came around the end of the Grand Ditch in a rainstorm after walking about 8 miles. It was getting cold as we entered the back side of the mountain range in the deep wilderness. We were glad to get camp set up, and we decided to call it a night early. I was sure that I could smell a bear but did not worry.

The next day we had planned a "down day" which ended being a hike up the mountain we camped under neath. At evening, after dinner, Kyle realized he had left his expensive sun glasses up on the mountain we had climbed that day and so off he went.

He came back down a couple hours later and we were safe in camp together again.

Jerry with Steve and Kyle after a long backpack trip around Never Summer Wilderness – real food.

The day after that, we hiked the back side of the mountain range. The mountains are named after clouds and it was truly beautiful country. At times, the trail was hard to find as we went up and over Baker Pass and down again. We went up and over a pass late in the afternoon. We called it "Not So Little Pass." It looked simple but it was a chore getting up to the top with our packs.

As we crested the pass, we could see black clouds ahead. We looked down the mountain side and saw the small lake where we were planning to spend the night. Kyle set the pace again going down the snowfield and across the rocks to the pristine setting.

What a beautiful place to spend the evening. The forest floor was so deep with a bed of needles it felt like a mattress. We slept well that night. That storm went north and around us, leaving us in peace that night.

The next day, we found a spring coming out of the mountain with sweet fresh water. We loaded up with good water and headed down the trail. As we came around the high shoulder of the mountain with great views, we looked down on the parking area and an old log cabin. There was the little red jeep Samurai we called "Sam".

When we finally came off that last mountain and were back to the jeep. Steve and I had discussed having a devotion each night to discuss an attribute of God.

In reality we were always exhausted and content to just sit and observe the fire in silence. At the end of the hide we looked at each other and the only word we could come up with which related to God that week was "BIG". He is a big God and his mountains are big and humble us.

He is also a Big God when it comes to blessings and keeping His children safe. Thank you, God.

Rich, Jerry, and Kyle backpack the Continental divide

This was a great backpack adventure on the back side of the Continental Divide in Rocky Mountain National Park. I packed a lot of fruit. On the first night, having climbed all day, I offered Kyle and Rich free fruit to renew their energy. Sometimes when you work hard in high altitudes, you feel more thirsty than hungry, so fruit satisfies your need for fluids and for energy.

We hiked up on top and across and back down to a beautiful campsite. Rich decided to spend the next day in peace and quiet at the camp while Kyle and I went up to a pristine lake we'd found on the map. Although the hike was tough, the trip was worth it. The location was incredible with tall flowers, and deer, and a beautiful lake and waterfall.

Kyle talked me into taking a short adventure cross- country. It started raining. The rocks were slippery, but we came down to another hidden lake lower down and followed the stream down to the camp. It was a beautiful few days in the mountains.

When we got down to civilization, I was offered a ride to the jeep, which was parked about 10 miles away at the entry to the trail up north, and drove back. Rich and Kyle met me in the diner on the boardwalk in Grand Lake for a big juicy hamburger, and many glasses of ice tea--nothing like a good meal when you come out of the mountains.

Thanking and praising God together

Wow Lord, we just love the high country beauty that you created. We enjoy the quiet and the incredible flowers up on Yankee Boy and Governor Basin in July, or the blue lupines on Last Dollar Road. We enjoy the waterfalls and colors of the fall and the variety of the rocks. We marvel at the seasons of Spring, Summer, and Fall, and even Winter. It is all beautiful, Lord. Most of all, we praise You for being the God who helps and strengthens and rescues us. Praise be to Your great and awesome name. We give you all the glory. Amen.

13. Blessing our children and grandchildren

"Those who live in the shelter of the Most High will find rest in the shadow of the Almighty. This I declare of the Lord: He alone is my Refuge, my place of safety; He is my God and I am trusting in Him. For He will rescue you from every trap and protect you from the fatal plague. He will shield you with His wings. He will shelter you with His feathers.

His faithful promises are your armor and protection. Do not be afraid of the terrors of the night, nor fear the dangers of the day, nor dread the plague that stalks in darkness, nor the disaster that strikes at midday. Though a thousand fall at your side, though ten thousand are dying around you, these evils will not touch you. But you will see it with your eyes; you will see how the wicked are punished.

If you make the Lord your refuge, if you make the Most High your shelter, no evil will conquer you, no plaque will come near your dwelling. He orders His angels to protect you wherever you go. They will hold you with their hands to keep you from striking your foot on a stone. You will trample down lions and poisonous snakes; you will crush fierce lions and serpents under your feet!

The Lord says, "I will rescue those who love me. I will protect those who trust in my name. When they call on me, I will answer, I will be with them in trouble. I will rescue them and honor them. I will satisfy them with long life and give them my salvation." Psalms 91

God blesses family and grandchildren

We are blessed, so we bless others

It was at our home church that a couple named Chuck and Mary Jo Larsen taught a class from the Ancient Path book about blessings. I remember reading the scripture several times from 1 Peter 3:9 that we are called to bless and not curse.

Because of that seminar, God put a passion into my heart to bless. I wrote blessings for my wife and children, which I prayed on a regular basis. Eventually, when our grandchildren came along, I also wrote prayers for them.

Speaking blessings is one of our privileges of a relationship with the Lord. Just as with any other spiritual gift, we have access to it, and are limited only by our understanding and application. I love to write blessings for others, and I encourage men to pray blessings over their wives and their children, and for wives to pray blessings over their husbands.

There is something truly special about someone communicating to you that they are praying for you specifically. May God bless you friend !

When a person is walking in the joy of the Lord, one of the ways they exhibit that joy is by blessing others. The great thing about that is that we are blessed as we are obedient, the recipient is blessed when God answers the prayer, and we may point others to Jesus Christ who is the ultimate one who blesses incredibly.

One of the studies our home church did in men's group was called *Letters from Dad* by Gregory Lee Vaughn. The night they started the seminar, there were fifty men of all ages in the room. One of the questions asked on the DVD was, "How many of you ever received a written blessing from your father?"

How many do you think raised their hand?

Twenty? Ten? Five ? No, Zero.

I looked at one of the group leaders and said, "We must change this."

As a result, Donna Kay and I pray blessings each day for each other and our family just as Jabez and Boaz and Moses prayed.

> *"Oh that You would bless me in all that I do, and keep me from all trouble and pain, and God granted him his request". 1 Chronicles 4:9*

Boaz comes to his workers "the Lord bless you" (Ruth 2) or "The Lord be with you". The workers respond back to Boaz, "the Lord bless you". Boaz to Ruth "May the Lord God of Israel, under whose wings you have come to take refuge, reward you fully". Naomi to Ruth "May the Lord bless the one who blessed you".

> *"May the Lord bless you and protect you. May the Lord smile on you and be gracious to you. May the Lord show you His favor and give you peace" Numbers 6: 22-26 (the priestly blessing)*

God blesses Jerry and Donna

Jerry and Donna taken at wedding of Kyle and Margie

Jere 9:23,24 _ "This is what the Lord says, "let not the wise man gloat in his wisdom, or the mighty man in his might, or the wise man in his wisdom. Let them boast in this alone; that they truly know me and understand that I am the Lord who is just and righteous, whose love is unfailing, and that I delight in these things, I, the Lord, have spoken!"

Isa 32:8 "Noble (honorable) men make noble (honorable) plans and by their noble (honorable) deeds they stand". NIV

What's in a name?

Jerry the "bridge builder". I can see ways I've lived up to my name by connecting with and reconciling others, giving a hand, bringing others to Jesus and encouraging them to stay with God. I have chosen to extend trust and lift up others rather than live with wounded feelings.

Donna my "beautiful lady". She truly is beautiful to me, inside and outside, precious, a joy and a blessing to me, a virtuous woman of Light and Life, a teacher and encourager to children and others. She is the love of my life and my soul mate.

1 Peter 3:4 " Be known for the beauty that comes from within, the unfading beauty of a gentle and quiet spirit, which is precious to God. That is the way the holy women of old made themselves beautiful. They trusted God and accepted the authority (protection) of their husbands."

God blesses Houle family - Cherri and Richard

"Oh that You would bless our children and grandchildren indeed, and enlarge their territories, that Your hand would be with them, and that You would keep them from evil, and that they might not cause pain " 1 Chronicles 4:9

At Disney World from left, Ben, Caris, Cherri, Rich, Glory and Hannah.

Cherri – beloved one of God - joyous life - God is Refuge - truly a front - runner by power of God - wonderful wife and mother - A home of peace in Jesus - Ministers to many - A warrior of Jesus.

Joel 3:16 "The Lord's voice will roar from Zion, and thunder from Jerusalem, and the earth and heavens will begin to shake. But to his people of Israel, the Lord will be welcoming refuge and a strong fortress."

Richard – leader like a lion - do God's will with compassion and courage – A man of honor and faithful friend and good listener. A servant of God.

"The Lord is my strength and my shield from every danger, I will trust in Him with all my heart. He helps me, and my heart is filled with joy. I burst out in songs of thanksgiving. The Lord protects His people and gives victory to His anointed. Save your people! Bless Israel, your special possession! Lead them like a shepherd, and carry them forever in your arms. Psalms 28:7-9

Ben – warrior of God - God is my refuge - Leader and servant - Fearless and compassionate - A joy to all - Loves Jesus and His Word.

"The Lord is a shelter for the oppressed, a refuge in times of trouble. Those who know your name trust in You., for you, O Lord, have never abandoned anyone who searches for you" Psalms 9:9

Ben is now in Belize and married to precious Raela. They serve the Children's home Laugh out Loud. The are a very beautiful godly couple.

Hannah – a tree of God - a lover of God, and beautiful in all His ways. Hannah - passion for healthy life - passion for healthy spiritual life.

"Blessed are those who trust in the Lord and have made the Lord their hope and confidence. They are like trees planted along a riverbank, with roots that read deep into the water. Such trees are not bothered by the heat or worried by long months of drought. Their leaves stay green, and they go right on producing delicious fruit. " Jeremiah 17:7

Caris – gift of God - she will be mighty in the service of the Lord - able to deal with complex things - She is quiet but wise in the Lord.

"I quietly wait before Go, for my salvation comes from Him. He alone is my rock and my salvation, my fortress where I will never be shaken" Psalms 62: 1,2

Glory – honoring God - God is using her to call others to a purified heart - A light of Jesus and blessing to all who know her. God's glory flows in her.

"Hezekiah did what was pleasing in the Lord's sight, just as his ancestor David had done. He said the Levites, Purify yourselves, and purify the temple of the Lord, the God of your ancestor. Remove all the defiled things. Hezekiah ordered the Levites to praise the Lord with psalms of David and Asaph the seer. So they offered joyous praise and bowed to worship." 2 Chronicles 29: 2,5,29.

God is so proud of this precious family that serves the Lord with all their heart, and so are we.

Bless them indeed, Lord. Thank You for each precious vessel serving with honor for Your Kingdom. Cherri and Rich have touched so many lives with their loving kindness and courage. They love the Word and love the Lord. We bless them all indeed. Amen.

God blesses English family - Jack and Wendy

From left ; Ryker, Amber, Jack, Wendy, Bailey and Bryce

Wendy – refreshing meadow, delight to God - God our refuge -Compassion to all. A blessed wife, mother, and daughter. Bless you always, dear Wendy, you are so precious to us all. May God restore to you a hundredfold.

> *"Those who trust in the Lord are as secure as Mount Zion; they will not be defeated but will endure forever. Just as the mountains surround and protect Jerusalem, so the Lord surrounds and protects His people, both now and forever." Psalms 125:1,2*

Jack – forgiving compassion - become all things to all men, to call to Jesus - leader and builder - generous and brave - man of God - loving husband and father – loyal and son of God.

> *"But the Lord is good; He has cut the cords used by the ungodly to bind me. The Lord's blessings be upon you; we bless you in the Lord's name." Psalms 129 4,8*

> *"When I pray, you answer me; you encourage me by giving me the strength I need. The Lord will work out His plans for my life-for your faithful love, O Lord, endures forever. Don't abandon me for you made me". Psalms 138*

> *"Search me, O God, and know my heart; test me and know my thoughts. Point out anything in me that offends You, and lead me along the path of everlasting life"*

Psalms 139 :23,24

This precious family is making a big difference eternally through the Vineyard Church in Ft Collins and Windsor, and expanding through their entire family. God is so proud of the English family as they serve the Lord with both compassion and joy. They all love to worship the Lord and love people.

Fun at YMCA Estes from left, Bryce, Bailey, Amber, and Ryker

Ryker – soldier of God - Ryker has become a gracious godly man and is in the process of getting college education and helping with worship leading.

You are highly esteemed by God and we bless you.

"I will proclaim the name of the Lord; how glorious is our God! He is the Rock; His work is perfect. He is a faithful God who does no wrong. The rock of our enemies is not like our Rock. " Deuteronomy 32:3,31

Amber – Colorful - talented and gracious. She is beautiful indeed. She is courageous and compassionate. Amber is a blessing to many to whom she ministers . Amber is a friend to animals.

"This is what the Lord says to Zerubbabel; It' s not by force, nor by strength, but by My Spirit, says the Lord Almighty. Do not despise small beginnings for the Lord rejoices to see the begin." Zechariah 3:6, 10

"Together they will wage war against the Lamb, but the Lamb will defeat them because He is Lord over all lords, and Kings over all kings, and His people are the called and chosen and faithful ones." Revelation 17:14

Bailey – refreshing breeze. We love you Bailey. You are beautiful inside and out. You are a servant and a leader. You lift others up. You lift up Jesus.

"Go out! Prepare the highway for any my people to return! Smooth out the road; pull out the boulders; raise the flag for the nations to see" Isaiah 62:10

Bryce – loyal to God - do not seek man's praise, but seek to know God. Thank you, Bryce, for being loyal to God in all you do. Also thoughtful and a friend to many.

"This is what the Lord says; Let not the wise man gloat in his wisdom, or the mighty man in his might, or the rich man in his riches. Let them boast in this alone; that they truly know me and understand that I am the Lord who is just and righteous, who love is unfailing, and that I delight in these things, I the Lord have spoken!" Jeremiah 9:23,24

We are so proud of each of these very precious jewels, and we believe in them and cherish them. God's plans are great for each of them and He will see it through to bless them indeed.

The love that this family has for others is amazing. There is a sweetness and gentleness that pervades their family. Jack is a builder and organizer, building up and helping energize others. Wendy is full of compassion with courage and great wisdom. She was a "soccer mom" going everywhere to help her four almost-grown children, who are now adults. Each of the children are becoming the vessels of honor just like their cousins at the Houle house. We praise you God for each of them!

God blesses beloved Tyrrell family - Serena and Isaac

"Oh that You would bless our children and grandchildren indeed, and "Oh that You would bless our children and grandchildren indeed, and enlarge their territories, that Your hand would be with them, and that You would keep them from evil, and that they might not cause pain " 1 Chronicles 4:9

Serena – peaceful as the dawn - devoted one - trusted-competent - dependable - integrity - creative - compassionate - discretion - endurance -grateful - homemaker-orderly - resourceful - virtuous - wise - servant of the Lord

"Jesus said, If you are thirsty, come to Me! If you believe in Me, come and drink! For the scriptures declare that rivers of living water will from out from within" John 7:38

"Happy are those who fear the Lord- all who follow His ways! You enjoy the fruit of your labor. How happy you will be! How rich your life! Psalms 128: 1,2

Isaac – laughter - truth - leads men and children - joyous, courageous, compassionate, resourceful, helpful, steadfast, loyal, patient, dependable, generous, gentle, wisdom, declarer of truth in power of God

> *"And the curtain of the temple was torn in two, from the top to the bottom. When the Roman officers who stood facing Him saw how he had died; he exclaimed, "Truly this was the Son of God!" Luke 15:38-39*

> *"If you obey the commands the Lord your God and walk in His ways, the Lord will establish you as His holy people as He solemnly promised to do. Then all the world will see that you are a people claimed by the Lord, and they will stand in awe of you. But if you refuse to listen to the Lord your God and do not obey.. then the curses will come and overwhelm you." Deuteronomy 28 9, 15*

Henry – future ruler - laughter - flexible to the need, and full of the Lord, secure, careful, alert, bold, forgiving, thoroughness, brings together unity

> *"Be humble and gentle. Be patient with each other, making allowance for each other's faults because of your love. Always keep yourselves united in the Holy Spirit, and bind yourselves together with peace". Ephesians 42,3*

> *"You will keep him in perfect peace all who trust in You, whose thoughts are fixed on You! Trust in the Lord always, for the Lord God is the eternal Rock." Jeremiah 26:3*

Wherever Isaac and Serena go, they bring the love and concern of Jesus Christ. The impact they made on those around them will bear eternal fruit. We salute them and stand with them always.

It was very hard to go to the mission field because of the need to raise support, and then it is difficult once the assignment is finished to do the re-entry to get settled and able to live back in America where things just do not go easy for people in terms of making a living. God bless them indeed.

Isaac, Serena and Henry in Rwanda serving with the Champions at the Orphanage under Victory Churches International.

God blesses beloved Swanson family - Kyle and Margie

"Oh that You would bless our children and grandchildren indeed, and enlarge their territories, that Your hand would be with them, and that You would keep them from evil, and that they might not cause pain " 1 Chronicles 4:9

Kyle – integrity - wise - a man of competence and courage, compassion and consistency, a leader and upright man who you can trust, walks with honor before God and man, frugal and fun

Micah 6:8 "what does God require, but to love mercy, do justly, and walk humbly before your God".

Margie – jewel - a precious lady who shines with Jesus and is a servant extra effort to be a homemaker, wife and mother, truly cherished .

1 Peter 3 cherished jewel of God with her quiet spirit Phil 4:6,7 peace that passeth understanding in Jesus .

Kyle and Margie are full of the Love of God and are a blessing to all who know them. They lift up others and they take time to enjoy life and the creation of God in their mountain trips.

Ruby - jewel of God - *Psalms 18:13 "He makes me sure-footed as a deer, leading me safely.. you have given me the supports me, your gentleness has kept me from slipping ".*

Luke - man of God – *2 Thessalonians 2:16 "May our Lord Jesus Christ comfort your hearts and establish them in every good word and work."*

Thank You, Lord, that You saved our Kyle and kept him safe all those years he was serving You and our country in his military missions. We are grateful that You found precious Margie as his beloved wife. We are thankful that You have blessed them with precious Ruby and Luke. We give You all the glory.

Thank You, Lord, that You kept Kyle through many mountain ventures and that You were there for him in time of need. We thank You that you have guided both him and Margie in their quest to find the path You have for them. We know that You can be trusted for what lies ahead.

Thank You, Lord, for rescuing me and Donna Kay when we were going to pick up Kyle at DIA on a cold icy morning as he returned from Afghanistan, as our car went spinning off I-25 and into the ditch. I said, "Help, Jesus" and Jesus helped us come right back out of the ditch and stop on the side of the road where we were able to rest and praise God.

We praise God that Kyle is safe at home with Margie and Ruby and Luke. We know You care about them, and we know that they are dedicated to a good life together as good parents and as helpers to others. God bless them indeed.

God blesses beloved family Gauthier – Christian and Erin

Erin Portal Gauthier came into our lives several years ago and we took her in as if she was one of our own daughters. She finished her degree at CSU for nursing and then came back to live with us for a while. We prayed for a good Christian man for her. God blessed her with Christian who has been a good husband and father of their precious children.

We bless Erin and Christian and pray blessings over them and over Rachel, Joanna, Bethany Joy, and Sarah. They are all very special to us and we love them as if they were our own.

Both Christian and Erin love the Lord and enjoy the mountains. They are great parents and an encouragement to both Donna Kay and me. Christian recently graduated from UNC as a Registered Nurse and does excellent work. They also have joined us in the Gideon ministry where they will use their gifts in reaching out to those who need Jesus.

Mama Erin, four girls (Sarah, Bethany, Joanna, Rachel), and Papa Christian

God blesses beloved Jerry and Donna on their 50th anniversary

What a marvelous party that our adult children and grandchildren threw for us. It was a most amazing time with many friends and family. They decorated the family room at Church of Good Shepherd and daughters Wendy, Cherri, Serena, and

Margie went over the top with food and drinks and invites and decorations, and even sang songs.

Richard and Cherri put together overhead pictures and music, and Kyle was MC asking people to come up and share. It was just fabulous.

We received a bucket of cards and gifts, and we will never forget this what a blessed occasion. God is good and we are thankful to all the family for the help and gifts and it sent us off on a trip later on.

This is the immediate family of Englishes : Wendy with Ryker,, Bailey and Bryce, Houles : Rich and Cherri with Hannah, Caris and Glory
Tyrrells with Isaac, Serena, and Henry
Swanson, Kyle and Margie
with Ruby and Luke
Jerry and Donna Kay.
Jack and Amber were in Africa and
Ben with Raela were in Belize

14. Our Heavenly Father blesses us

"I will rescue you from those you fear so much. Because you trusted in me. I will preserve your life and keep you safe. I, the Lord have spoken!" Jeremiah 39:17

"See how much our heavenly Father loves us, fore He allows us to be called His children, and we really are ! 1 John 3:1

"To all who are thirsty I will give the springs of the water of life without charge! All who are victorious will inherit all these blessings". Revelations 21: 6,7

Our Heavenly Father blesses those who seek Him

The truth of God, the Father's love for us, is so vital because no matter how hard we try, we aren't able to be the ideal parent for our children and grandchildren.

Recently, while sharing a word of testimony and testaments with students on a college campus, a girl named Candy told me she did not have a father.

Seeing that she was upset, I told her, "Yes, you do, and He absolutely adores you--He is your heavenly Father and He loves you. He has great plans for you, and He will never leave or forsake you."

She seemed to accept what I was saying, and left looking a lot happier than just a few minutes before.

Pastor Rob Strouse at our home church keeps trying to make sure we all understand the truth of our Heavenly Father's love and commitment to us as His children.

Listed below are blessings from our Heavenly Father--simple truths in my life and in Donna Kay's life. May you find them an encouragement to you.

- **My heavenly Father calls me home, forgives me, and heals my wounds.**

The story of the lost and wounded son reflects the Father's love for us as we come home to Him. (Luke 15). Our Lord has come to heal the broken-hearted and give us a garment of praise. He even calls us trees. (Isa 61). "Yet in this one thing I hope; it is my portion--that God's mercies are new every morning. Lam 3:24,25.

God made a covenant of kindness and fulfilled it in Jesus. (Isaiah 54).

Jesus says "Come unto me all you that labor and are heavy laden and I will give you rest". Matthew 11:28-30.

- **The heavenly Father's power in us through Jesus Christ–Savior and Lord.**

There is an enemy that promotes sin and self, who wants to kill and destroy. Our only hope is Jesus Christ (John 10:10). God has provided a lasting solution in Jesus if we believe and love God more than our darkness (John 3:16-17)

If we truly want to obey our Father, we join those in Acts 2:38 "repent and be baptized" and blessings abound. We then become disciples of Jesus, (Matthew 5-7), and we call others to be disciples of Jesus (Matt 28:18).

- **My heavenly Father longs to restore and help and be my Shepherd**

"The Lord was my support and brought me to a safe place, He delivered me and delighted in me". Psalms 18.

"The Lord is my shepherd I shall not want, He lets me lie down in green pastures, He restores my soul". Psalms 23.

"Delight in the Lord and feed on His faithfulness and He will give you the delights of your heart", Psalms 37.

"Now may the God of hope fill you with all joy and peace in believing and you may abound in Hope by the power of the Holy Spirit". Romans 15:13.

- **My heavenly Father provides a unique Heart Blessing, affirmed in brothers**

God says in Jeremiah 29:11: "My thoughts for you are for good, not evil, and for a good hope and future."

However, we must choose to give God our whole heart day by day and not be pulled back and forth with the world. God wants a heart that is true to Him, (Psalms 15). When we are truthful with God and our brothers, the blessings abound.

"We are called to bless and not curse" 1 Peter 3.

" Encourage each other" Heb 10:25.

"Be subject to one another out of reverence for Christ " Eph 5:22,

We are members of the family of God, (Eph 4). We all have different combinations of gifts, passions, and experiences that we are to use to God's glory and the good of the Body, (Romans 12). We should be considerate of our brothers and sisters as to their building up, (Romans 14), and not just our own needs. Our brothers and sisters can teach us much if we will learn but we must teach humbly and wisely,

The Lord's servants must not quarrel but must be kind to everyone. They must be able to teach effectively and be patient with difficult people. They should gently teach those who oppose the truth. Perhaps God will change those people's hearts, and they will believe the truth. Then they will escape from the devil's trap. For they have been held captive by him to do whatever he wants." 2 Timothy 2 : 24-26 "

- **My heavenly Father will give me living power in His Word and Holy Spirit**

"Blessed is the man who meditates on the Word of God-he shall be a tree, successful in life", Psalms 1.

" All Scripture is given by inspiration of God and is profitable for doctrine, reproof, correction and instruction that the man of God might be complete and thoroughly equipped for every good work", 2Tim 3 .

"There is now no condemnation for those in Christ Jesus, for those that walk in the Spirit", Romans8:1.

"The fruit of the Spirit is love, joy, peace, patience, kindness, goodness, faithfulness, gentleness, and self-control. against such there is no law. If we live in the Spirit, let us walk in the Spirit " Galatians 5:22-26.

We become warriors for the Lord by His Spirit of power.

"We have not been given the spirit of fear, but of power, love and wisdom "2 Tim 1:7.

- **My heavenly Father is able. He wins, we win with Him!**

My Father is so big and able to do all things through us to His glory.

"Have you not seen, have you not heard, The everlasting God, the Lord, the Creator of heaven and earth does not faint or grow weary. Those who wait upon the Lord shall renew their strength, they shall mount up with wings of eagles and run and not grow weary and walk and not faint". Isaiah 40.

"He is able to do abundantly more than we think or ask in Jesus." Ephesians 3:20.

- **Praise be to our Heavenly Father**

Heavenly Father, how can we reject Your loving gift in Jesus Christ? We cannot. We give our lives to You in service, desiring to rest and be restored day by day because of your divine Spirit in us of power, love, joy, peace, wisdom, and wit. We welcome Your Spirit and rise each morning to thank You, our loving Father and our great and awesome God. Praise be to Your name. Amen.

15. Heavenly Father blesses families

"Praise the Lord! Happy are those who fear the Lord. Yes, happy are those who delight in doing what He commands. Their children will be successful everywhere: An entire generation of people will be blessed: Psalms 112 : 1,2

God blesses our extended family

"Grant me purity of heart that I might honor you" Psalms 86:11

Written by Jerry on one of their anniversaries

A girl from Kansas

Born as a surprise to the Smiths one day,

She grew up shy in country ways.

She went to college, by now a beauty,

She met Jerry, not a duty.

They walked and talked, and one day kissed,

And from that day love never missed.

In September they wed and off they went,

To begin a life with mountains and tent.

One child, then more, and before you know it

Years go by and their love shows it.

Not much in bank, or fame, or plaques,

But they celebrate memories that come back.

If you asked them the secret to this good success,

They'd say, "Keep your eyes on Jesus and use good sense ".

Donna Kay's folks came originally from Kentucky to Kansas and they raised sheep for some years then switched to cattle. Her grandparents families were Smith and Bemis. Her siblings are brother John Park III and sister Betty Jean. They lived where the Quivera Wildlife Reserve is now, and the pond near their old homestead is named Park Smith Pond. Her father was known as a man of integrity, intelligence, compassion, a hard worker, a builder, and courage. A man of God.

Donna's kin begin with father John Park Smith II and mother Hollis Minnie Bemis. They had three children; Betty Jean, John Park III, and Donna Kay. Betty married Allen Keeler whose children include Karen (married to Jim Crane), Kenny (married to Jackie), and Kim (married to David Gustafson). John Park III married Glenda and their boys are Shawn (married to Sherry), and Shelby (married to Lora).

And of course, Donna Kay married me and we just talked about all our wonderful children and grandchildren.

At the writing of the book, Betty Keeler remains in Hutchinson and her children and grandchildren are in either Hutchinson, Kansas or Oklahoma. Glenda Smith is remarried to Charley Giles as John Park III went home several years ago. Both Shawn and Shelby and their families live in Texas.

Donna's parents took people in and helped those in need. They were hardworking farmers-ranchers who experienced hard times and went through the depression years, and certainly knew how to get by and do without. It seemed there was nothing her dad could not do on the farm: fixing things around the house, working with the animals, harvesting all kinds of crops, raising just about any farm animal, hunting, and also raising catfish.

Their garden was notable with many vegetables, enough to can and eat and plenty to share. Most of the time after church, Park and Hollis opened the trunk of their car to give what they had: tomatoes, beans, and many times cantaloupe and watermelon. Yum!

Donna's mom was an excellent cook and used to fix'n for plenty. I remember one time that we sat down and I saw the platter of pork chops (my favorite) on the table. I noticed there were nine chops on the platter and ten people sitting around the table. As we bowed to say grace, I was wondering how we were going to resolve this situation.

After grace, there was a big commotion around the table and everyone was going for a pork chop. It kind of embarrassed Donna Kay,

.....but I enjoyed the two I got.

One of my favorite memories is putting up hay in the summer. It was hard work and hot, but it was so good to sit down and enjoy pork chops, mashed potatoes, green beans, fresh tomatoes, and dessert, and never gain a pound. It was also so easy to sleep at night.

One of the experiences when we were first married and visiting Donna's folks, was a winter blizzard that knocked out the electricity. There wasn't much else to do, so we enjoyed playing dominos by candlelight.

We made sure to go back and forth to visit Donna's folks each year. We enjoyed our trips to Kansas and out time there. Despite what folks say, Kansas isn't all flat land and corn fields. I think the most precious memories are about the people, not about what we did.

In fact, I struggle to remember a lot of where we went. It was always the people who made the trip memorable. There are many, many, many precious memories. Park and Hollis went home to be with the Lord. They lived a godly life for

Jesus with a clear conscience before God and man. We miss them, but they are always with us in Spirit.

After Donna's parents passed, Donna's sister, Betty, became the hostess for all to come for Thanksgiving. It was special for many years after the parents died, and Betty always had room at her table for our family as well as Glenda and her family when they could make it from Texas. There was good food, playing football, and sitting around singing gospel songs later. Love always abounded at the Smith and Keeler homes. Several people became like family including Steve and Patty Sears in Hutch.

All the family got along and enjoyed each other. There was a Spirit of peace with the Lord. None went hungry, nor were any neglected.

Donna Kay's parents Park and Hollis

Betty (Donnas' sister) , Kim (her niece), and Donna Kay
Taken in the church at Hutchinson , Kansas

Story told by my Dad (written while at York annual roundup)

Memories of the Forties - when the nation was drawn into the Big One, World War Two. I was a young married man who was getting quite well established up on a farm and was thrilled when I was able to rent a farm to operate on my own. We were blessed with a good crop so were able to purchase a tractor for $1000, and move up from farming with horses. Our twelve milk cows, a few hogs, and some chickens helped us to have a good living. We felt we had a good start toward freedom from debt and were looking forward to the birth of our second child (that's me).

Uncle Sam sent me greetings, saying he had other plans for me. This was a big disappointment, but I had no choice in the matter. Having passed the physical with flying colors, I was soon off to Camp Maxey near Paris, Texas. I put my wife, small daughter, and new baby boy in a house in town that I bought for $1800, after our farm sale. They would live there until I return.

My training was tough. The hard work on the farm helped me to be better able to handle it than some of the city boys were. I was happy when my little family came to spend the summer near the camp. We couldn't be together much and when we could, I was tired but so thrilled to have them near.

They gave my company a two weeks leave before taking us on a two weeks train ride. This ended in Oregon where, after one more week, they trucked us to Camp Lawton in Washington. After a week there, they shipped us to Okinawa. We were "treated" to a typhoon before the week was out. During this time, we were never dry. Winds 165 miles plus per hour with driving sheets of rain continued for three days and nights. One didn't stand against it. If we moved, we crawled.

The war was over, so it was our job to clean up the Island. We dug trenches and bulldozed the dead into them for burial. We lived in tents, used outdoor latrines, and a water truck gave us showers in the open. We swam in the ocean each day. I was put in charge of a warehouse that dispensed parts for equipment and vehicles. It wasn't hard - Japanese prisoners working under me tried hard to please. It was rewarding to have risen from private to Sergeant during my tour of duty for the dear old U.S.A. We hurried home, taking only 20 days to sail home instead of 27 days that it had taken to go. I appreciate the expense free two years of my life that Uncle Sam gave me, and as to hankering to do it again — well, NO THANKS !!!

Another story told by my Dad, Ray Swanson

One spring day in 1927 I came walking 2 miles from school. My dad said to me, I have something to show you in the barn. My heart jumped, could it be a pony which I had hoped to have some day, as I had grown to like horses very much. At that time farming was done with horses. In coming to the barn I was having a hard time not to run but to walk with Dad. He opened the door. There was the most beautiful pony I had ever seen- a pretty Dapple Grey, as she got older she turned white at 8 years old weighing 800 lbs. She was pretty big for a small boy, but I always found a way to get on her. We became good friends. Learning to ride was so much fun. I rode to get cows in for milking, also sometimes to school in the summers my cousin and I would go for rides as he got a pony also.

Bell later became the family pony, as I was the oldest of 14 children and left to work away from home at the age of 13.

In the year of 1935 there was a lot of snow. I can remember many days we could not get out of the place, as we lived in the hills. One morning it was decided that I would take the pony and go to Swede Home, a little town about 5 miles away to get some things we needed. So I arrived there about noon and got the things mother had written down. Meanwhile the wind had come up blowing the snow so I could not see at all. Harold, the store man, said you can't go home now as I had to go into the wind. I said sure I can. My pony will take me home. I did by holding on to her tail for 5 miles. We arrived home safely and I can still see her steps in the snow - I stepped in them as we went on our way home.

A real trusty horse to have was my pony Belle!!

A story told by my mother Donna Pearl Hinton Swanson

Best quencher of thirst. How good that water tasted on a hot July day! When first pumped from the well by the back door. It was clear and cold. That is, if it was pumped slow and easy, it wouldn't have but a trace of sand in the bottom of the bucket, after a while. Now and again Dad would pull the pump (pipes attached) and sand-pump the well to remedy the sediment problem. The long-handled tin dipper would give the teeth a chill if you weren't careful when drinking. How fortunate there was a drain that carried water from the kitchen sink to a cesspool at the west edge of the the yard! We carried water in the house but didn't carry it out.

One of the best things about getting back after some time away from home was a refreshing drink of the best water under God's heavens ! No where else and no time since have I ever tasted water so good.

Another story told by my mother Donna Pearl - Childhood memories.

One of my early childhood memories is of frolicking on the flour mill floor after the rest of the building had been dismantled. It was such a huge area four feet or so above the ground. I could march or skip, run or jump or I could just take a leisurely stroll giving my doll a ride in her buggy. I knew this mill floor would soon be taken, too. Dad was using lumber salvaged from the mill in the erecting of our new barn.

The creek made more noise where it flowed past the mill. There were still huge old iron slabs, iron slabs, broken chunks of iron wheels and such, where the creek had been damned to furnish energy by water wheel for making flour. Water sloshed and foamed making its way through. I have a scar over my hip bone that reminds me debri was still there 6 or 7 years later. I struck it while swimming with some cousins when I was 11. What fun to splash into the water from slippery mud-slides we made along the creek bank! Medicine Creek furnished fun-time doings for the gal from the Old Mill Stream.

One more story from my mother – Daytime darkness

Who remembers the Dirty Thirties better than I? Little drifts of fine dust formed at every crack where even light could peek through. It covered the window sills, thresholds, and every object in the house collected it, and quickly we would wash the table clean and carry dishes to the table and hear that gritty sound as you put them in place.

Only once did I take a chance and cut across Bill Reed's alfalfa field! (My Dad could call him Bill but on "Mr Reed" was allowed to cross my lips). And I was never permitted to make tracks on his property. My friend Darlene, was with me. Dust filled our nostrils and because of dust and darkness we couldn't see the way. School had just let out and it should have been daylight but clouds of dirt darkened the sun. Darlene stopped and screamed because she thought we were lost. I took her by the shoulders and shook her hard while I screamed at her. Then she let me take her hand and lead her on home with me. We were safe from the dirt storm! I know my guardian angel guided me.

Thanking God indeed

Yes, Lord, we thank you for this precious legacy in the life of Park and Hollis Smith and all of the good life they lived and all the good treasures that go on through the kin. All the children and grandchildren have good memories. We pray continued blessings on all who follow. In Jesus' name. Amen.

Blessings to my family

I was born to Raymond Lester Swanson and Phyllis Ilene Esau Swanson in Osceola, Nebraska, which is north and east of York. Jerry's dad, Ray, was a rodeo rider and had no fear. He was the oldest of 14 and left home at the age of 13 to work on a farm in Iowa.

My mother, Phyllis, died in January 1966, and then Ray married Laura Lee, and then she died about five years later, and then Ray married Donna Pearl Johnson Hinton, and they were married over forty years. Ray died on April 5, 2010 in North Platte having lived over 92 years as a very committed Christian and friend to many.

Donna Pearl and Ray Swanson brought great unity to both of their families

Ray was a dedicated man of God who loved family and God above all his personal pleasures. He was always committed to reading the Word and living an upright life and lived a life of integrity, which blesses all of us.

A man named Ray

You meet some people in your life
Who are not the normal type,
Ones you note as they cross your way
People who really brighten your day.
Ray is one who was unique,
He didn't complain or miss a beat
Life was full of things to do,
And Ray would never say "no" to you.
He loved to work and help and mend,
He fixed a fence and patched a man

He had a faith that was strong,
And was never known to do a wrong.
He'd lend a hand, he'd bare his heart
And never shied from doing his part.
He could break a horse and feed the cows
And fix'em up and take'em down
He cared for mom and all us kids
The Hand of God in all he did.
And still had time to be a friend,
A loving dad until the end.

Love, your privileged son, Jerry

Front : Jimmy with Ray middle and Ted on right
Back ; Phyllis, Rosalie, and Maxine year 2010

Ray's siblings were: Jean Margaret, Elmer LeMoyne, Warren Richard, Theodore Wayne, Phyllis Ann, Norman Dean, Dennis Lewis, Shirley Mae, Rosalie Marie, Rex Leonard, Larry LeRoy, Maxine Arnetta, and Jim Lee.

At the writing of this book those still alive include: Phyllis Schick in Ohio, Rosalie Paulson in Oregon, and youngest brother Jimmy Swanson with his family near Polk, Nebraska.

My grandparents were Elmer Frederick Swanson and Ethel Anna Marie Lundgren. Jerry's great grandparents (Swanson side) came from Sweden. His grandfather, Elmer, organized the annual Swanson Rodeo in Central City and Buffalo Bill came to that rodeo. Ray was a farmer, rancher and Rodeo rider.

Jerry's grandparents – Marie and Elmer Swanson

My dad, Ray, tells the story of going to Swede's home for groceries one winter day. It was several miles from their home. Ray said the storeowner said, "You better stay here, Ray, a blizzard is now blowing outside and very dangerous." Ray said, "No, I will go home." I asked my dad many years later, "What did you do?" Dad said, "No problem. I just took hold of the tail of my pony and he knew the way home in the blizzard."

One of Dad's closest cousins, Vernon Swanson, who is married to Arlene, lived in Dallas, Texas with their daughter Susan Swanson Miller married to Larry Miller. I also stay in touch with Jimmy Swanson's daughter Kim married to Tom Gless. My dad used to share the story of how he rode his white pony and met with Vernon. They were like brothers.

I have many fond memories of Vernon and Arlene. As we lived near them in Lincoln, Nebraska, they got together to enjoy hamburgers and the parents played games. They went to the Church of Christ in Lincoln. They were exceptionally kind and truly interested in Jerry and his siblings. Thank you.

The picture below was taken of me and my brother and two sisters at Kearney Camp get together.

Picture below of Rona, Jerry, Rod, and Judie at Camp

Judie (my older sister) married Larry Brewster from Oklahoma and they live in Worland, Wyoming. Their children include (Chris married to Tim McGee) in Worland, Jay (married to Stephanie) and lives in Malibu, CA, Kelly (married to John

Osborne) living in Oklahoma City, and Jeff (married to Lynda) living in Casper, Wyoming.

Rona (my youngest sister) is married to Sam, and they have daughter Sara married to Mitch. Son Caleb is married to Melissa and they have three precious daughters - Rebekah Faith, Emma Grace, and Arabelle Marie. Sam and Rona's other daughter, Rebekah, died January 13, 2004, but still lives in all our hearts. My favorite saying of Rebekah was, "We are all angels until someone ruffles our feathers." Rona is a writer and insurance agent and blesses so many.

Arabelle Marie, Emma Grace, and Rebekah Faith

My stepfamily from my stepmother, Laura Lee, included children Jim Lee, Jerry Lee, and Ed (and Dee) Lee living in Kearney, Nebraska.

Rod my beloved younger brother married Connie Ford in 1972 in Solana Beach, California. They had known each other since they were 16. They lived in Southern California for 20 years and have now lived in Northern California for 20 years. All Rod's children are now married with his youngest, Benjamin married in May of 2016. They are blessed to have all their children and grandchildren living in the Bay Area. The photos below are from Benjamin's wedding.

Rod Swanson and children 2016
Left to right; Emily, Benjamin, Christina (Ben's bride)
Connie, Rod, Amanda

Rod Swanson Whole Family 2016
Left to right; the Fitzpatrick's Joe, Reilly, Emily (Swanson), Lily, Rod and Connie Swanson, Benjamin Swanson and Christina, Christina's parents Andrea and Sandy Perry, the Dowd's - Geoff, Amanda (Swanson), Oscar and Ray (named after Ray Swanson).

My stepfamily from my precious stepmother, Donna Hinton, includes her children who, of course, became Ray's also. They are Deloit Hinton (with Carol) living in California; Bernita (with husband John) who live near Curtis, Nebraska; Loraine lives in Nebraska; Everett married Ann and they live in Hastings, Nebraska; Laurence and Tamara Hinton live in North Platte, Nebraska and they cared for Mom and Dad for the last 20-plus years.

Picture below of Laurence and Tamara's family. We have been family for 40 years and deeply love all our Hinton family. They are all very honorable and godly family.

Laurence and Tamara Hinton and their family

God bless all the Swanson-Smith-Esau-Hinton family kin, and of course, all the families that follow.

My grandparents from my mother Phyllis's side were Charles Roy Esau born May 17, 1885 with wife Anna Lou Bruen Esau born December 5, 1891. Charles was born coming over on ship from the Prussian revolution. Great-grandfather was Jacob Esau and great-great- grandfather, Igor Esau from Ukraine. This is of interest since I did some mission work in Ukraine, not knowing I had roots there. Slava Bogu! (Praise the Lord!)

Anna Lou Bruen, my grandmother through my mother Phyllis's family, was daughter to David L. Bruin. His first wife died and he remarried the lady who took care of the house, named Maudie Black. They lived in Albion, Nebraska. (Source from Phil Esau.)

Perhaps because of my distant familial relationship to the Arapahoe, I deeply appreciate Dennis Carlin and the ministry Nation to Nation that works with the Lakota Nation in South Dakota. Missionary and Pastor Dennis Carlin is faithful in this wonderful ministry. He is a true friend and brother and makes a big impact as he and wife Leala continue to conduct a radio program out of KILI radio in Porcupine, South Dakota while they work with a church in Kyle, South Dakota. God bless this ministry.

God, help us to speak straight with love.

"You must speak straight so that your words may

go as sunlight into our hearts." Cochise Chiricahua Chief

My mother, Phyllis, had several siblings, including Earl Esau, who married Margaret and lived in Ohio most of his life. Earl's children are Phillip (with wife Emily) who still live in Ohio, daughter Karen Esau, and son David Esau.

Phyllis also had a sister Darlene Esau who married into the Dunkle family, and then Phyllis's youngest brother Ken Esau. His daughters are Reba, DeAnna Raines, and Dona Songbondi. I am not sure of all the Dunkle kin, but I see some on Facebook.

DeAnna and her husband Jerry Rains live in Denver, and their children include Michael and Kendra. Dona and Lahai Songbondi live in Denver. Both DeAnna and Dona were adopted by my parents from the Ken Esau family.

My present mother, Donna Pearl Hinton Swanson, tells us that when you take into account her side of the family and Ray, my dad's, side of the family, that our recent granddaughter, Ruby Annabelle, was their one hundredth descendant. Praise the Lord.

Donna and I deeply appreciate Donna Pearl, my mother, still living in North Platte past the age of 90 and a blessing to all of us. She is an exceptional Christian lady who has kept in touch with all the family for years. She had written individual birthday card for each member of her extended family.

Both my mom and my dad lived lives dedicated to the Lord Jesus and set a good example in Jesus.

Family Gatherings

There were so many times over fifty years that Donna and I went home to the Smith and Swanson parents and kin. These were good times and good memories. We are so grateful for keeping in touch, not only with our parents, but also siblings and cousins and such. The older we get, the more we seem to care about our kin. We always went with blessings and prayers and tried to build bridges. Most all of our family is committed to Jesus Christ which makes our reunions sweet.

On the Swanson side, our visits to the Swanson and Hinton families were at Kearney Youth Camp. It was a fun place to go since there is a sandpit where everyone can cool off on a hot summer day. Some years it was 110 degrees. The kids and grandkids alike loved to swim or go on canoes around the lake, and there was always lots of good food. Sometimes, if the weather held up, we'd even have a hayride.

*Think this was taken about 1987,
at a Swanson-Hinton-Smith family reunion at Kearney
Camp.*

Those Swanson-Hinton reunions went on for thirty years and we had a lot of good times. One benefit of a family reunion is getting to know all your extended family. Once we knew them better, we try to keep in touch. Laurence and Tamara led us in another reunion this past summer. It was small but great. Each of our adult children families are growing up and it was hard to round everyone up. Some of the older adults don't travel much, and from year to year, others "went home" We have learned life is short; enjoy it while you can.

This year, we took Caris and Bryce with us. We had a terrific time at the Nebraska Youth Camp, which is operated by Church of Christ. The cabins are rustic and the showers are rustic and it is sandy like a beach, but is a wonderful place. We want to also acknowledge two people who we think of as almost members of the family: Harold and Dena Tandy. They have who cooked for us for years. They work at York College and are very special servants of the Lord. God bless the Tandys'.

We also have gatherings on the Smith side. Our visits usually take place at the farm, which is a special treat. Although life there is definitely slower and more laid-back, there was always something going on: relaxing and playing games while munching on a bowl of popcorn was a favorite pastime. Grandma Hollis had a game called POLLYANNA that was fun, and sometimes we played dominos, and many times we just visited and caught up on the news.

At Camp from left ; Donna Kay, Rona, Judie, Kelly and Connie. So many good memories at summer Camp.

Church family too – many Churches

Wow, Jerry and Donna have had so many friends through many churches over the years: Logan Street in Denver (Jim and Ann Thompson and also Larry and Kathy Long were neighbors); University Blvd in Denver (Selbys, McKnights, Wards, Driggers, Scibas); Southside in Lexington,Kentucky (Goughs, Cooks, Baxters); Bellevue in Washington (Jewetts, McClures, Fletchers, Meadors, Mortensons, Allens, Millers, Foxes and great neighbors Norm and Kathy Grauman), Cloverdale in Indiana (Parkers, Witkanaks, Nicholsons, McClane, Schroer, Fites), Salem Road, Rochester, MN – mention in another place, and then finally back to Colorado.

Church family – Hutchinson Church of Christ

We were blessed abundantly with love and kindness from all the precious folk at Hutchinson including family members, friends, and friends in Christ.

Kim and David Gustafson with Brody. They always show us warm hospitality. Kim is Donna Kay's niece and David serves as an elder at Hutch Church

Church family – Loveland Good Shepherd Church

We have now been at Good Shepherd Church, Loveland for twenty-two years.

I have special memories of my mens' group in the congregation growing together: Robert Tholl, Ron Damon, David Cook, Dave Campbell, Perry Williams, Ken Hoornbeek, Lee Rosen, Allen Colvin, and Tim Wadham. It is so good to have men who you can meet with regularly and pray with. Fellowship with faithful brothers is vital if we want to grow in Christ to be refined for God's highest purposes.

Over the years, several men have led our men's group, including: Greg Muhonen, Mark Bower, Chuck Layman, Dick Hansen, Jeff Monson, Tom Bloom and Phil Brewster, and sometimes Pastor Kent Hummel who were all godly men. When you are around godly men who are willing to be humble, authentic, and real, you learn by observing what they do and how they live, and together you learn how to walk in the Spirit from reading and studying the Word of God together.

"As iron sharpens iron, a friend sharpens a friend." Proverbs 27:17

There were several couples who were instrumental to our spiritual growth either by their example or service or sharing words of the Lord over the years we have been at Good Shepherd church:

Bob and Pat Heiser, Dennis and Sondra Merk, Chuck and Mary Hill, Bob and Diana Tholl, Ron and Geri Damon, Dennis and Sandra Merk, Larry and Claire Rideout, Royal and Julie Rich, David and Lisa Rodgers, Kent and Jan Hummel, Rob and Shirley

Strouse, Tom and Wanda Davis, Dick and Ann Hansen, Dave and Dena Trumbo, Tom and Jana Tyrrell, Howard and Diane Farqhuar, Mark and Cindy Schilling, Russ and Connie Jones, Dave and Pat Cook, Bob and Diane Montgomery, Phil and Belinda Brewster, Bert and Patty Morrison, Jim and Robin Parker, Bob and Jan Black, Dave and Vernie Campbell, Bill and Dee Carrillo, Don and Jean Maggard, Greg and Pam Muhonen, Dave and Judy Goltz, Kurt and Kate Garland, Blake and Kristin Bush, Adam and Marsha Heiser, Ron and Kathy Herman, Chuck and Elaine Layman, Jim and Cathy Rudolph, Tom and Debby Green, Paul and Mary Scott, Tim and Susan Bebo, David and Kathy Berry, Conrad and Lori Boland, Paul and Valerie Bakes, Erik and Jody Brolsma, Dennis and Diana Bruns, Dan and Anne Clark, Michael and Denise Coffman, Chris and Anna Cozza, Howard and Nancy Croft, Bonnie DeManche, Mick and Julie Echelberger, Robert Elsey, John and Stephanie Larsen, David and Jennifer Hanes, Dave and Leanne Hoffman, George and Lisa Holling, Dick and Dixie Huff, Ray and Alice Hummel, Jon and Annie Hummel, Bill and Linda Johnson, Mike and Carrie Keirns, Larry and Rebecca Kawa, Tim and Sandra Lebeda, Jim and Marian Lewis, Steve and Terry Lewis, Jon and Maura Link, Mike and Margery Marquez, Jeff and Cindy McCauley, Karen Mendoza, Shirleen Milon, Dottie Mommer, Jeff and Pam Monson, Sandra Montgomery, Tom and Melissa Moore, Randy and Brenda Moore, Chad and Terri Morrison, Roger and Katie Myers, Don and Mary Nadow, Mike and Amy Nappa, Brian and Cheryl Wong, Greg Oliver, Don and Linda Pacas, Jean Porter, Lee and Penny Rosen, Matt and Cindy Porter, Susan Propp, Mike and Lesa Ramirez, Joyce Rezac, Stan and Maggie Ross, Glenn and Mercella Rowe, Ray and Kelly Sanchez, Bud and Tracy Saults, Greg and Kathleen Seja, Russ and Joni Sellars, Brian and Danel Lins, Kathy Simmons, Zach and Demi Smith, Carl Smith, Walt and Marlyn Smith, Bill Smith, Lori and Lynn Stauffer, Doug and Gwen Stephenson, David and Emily Straw, Mike and Lisa Swanson, Mike and Lacy Tonniges, Steve and Cindy Towne, Doug and Valerie Towne, Drew and Ellen Travota, Margaret Trujillo, Gene and Joyce Van Tress, Bryan and Angie Vincent, Tim and Cheri Wadham, Fred and Kathryn Wadam, Dee Waldron, Corina Lane, Eric and Sherri Weinmaster, Sallie Westfall, Ward and DeAnn Westfall, Jason and Rachel Williams, Perry and Kim Williams, Brian and Lisa Winbourn, Jerry and Peggy Windsor, Chris and Summer Woodward, Justin and Monica Yates, and our own Richard and Cherri Houle, and Isaac and Serena Tyrrell, and Kyle Swanson.

All remain in our hearts and prayers that God's plans may be completed in each life, and that God would bless those who blessed us.

Forgive us if we left off a name. Many years, many faces, and at age 70, the old memory is not as good, which makes it even more important we record this precious list before more names fade.

We are blessed to have friends in many churches and we rejoice at the common bond for those who seek and walk with Jesus and with His Word.

Bind us together Lord, with cords that cannot be broken.

I love to build bridges of peace in Jesus as I kneel at the foot of the cross. Humility and Purity in Jesus brings down the walls of pride and offense, and leads us to walk humbly before God and our fellowman.

Prison ministry – Warriors for Christ

A great memory picture for me is when the prison group, Warriors for Christ, did a yard event in Ark Valley Prison. Sitting beside me on the front row was Bass who had been one of the Muslim gang leaders, but was now a Christian. We were singing together the Promise Keepers song "Godly Men".

Grant Lord, that we all would seek to be godly men and walk in purity, integrity and honor to the glory of Jesus our King.

Prison ministry calls for complete authenticity, with humility and courage. The men can truly see through you. I am deeply grateful to Dave Cook who helped start the ministry and then Jeff Monson, Phil Brewster, and Richard Houle who were the "cord of three", the pioneers who set up the foundation.

In recent years, Ron Damon, Phil Brewster, Bob Tholl, Bert Morrison, Sergio Plaza, and Jeff Monson have kept the ministry going. Ron could name all those who still participate all over the state. The men in prison deeply appreciate the faithful support.

Gideon family – brothers and sisters in Jesus

Donna and I have served for 30 years in the Gideon ministry. Sometimes that service has been a sacrifice, as we don't receive any compensation for our work. The ministry's goal is reaching the lost, spreading the Word, and raising funds for more Bibles.

What kept us inspired to make the sacrifice of time and money and service is that the system works. God's Word is not just a book, seldom read. It is the Living Word of God, and it changes lives through the power of the Holy Spirit.

Lord God, please stir a revival for people to return with a passion to the Word to know the ways of God and honor Him in purity and peace.

I mention the following names as some of the many in the Gideons International ministry whom we love and serve with:

Gary and Lisa Coram, Fred and Dena Urben, Allen and Terry Huth, Don and Maxine Hunter, Gordy and Patty Kelley, Howard and Carla Copeland, Jan and JJ Bertholf, Bob and Sherry Carter, Richard and Linda Dykstra, Patrick and Donna Schlachter, Larry and Jan Doolen, Ken and Diane Goldsberry, Stan and Irene Attleson, Dave and Triana Burrill, Keith and Kelli Couch, Ron and Jeri Damon, Bob and Diana Tholl, Glen and Donna Steelman, Stan and Donna Versaw, Jim and Mary Waddle, Mike and Kay Argall, Albert Avery, Elliott and Sherry Hays, Lloyd and Mary

Stone, Fred and Debbie Sutton, Ken and Bernice Rutz, Earl and Helen Harper, Jody and Susan Smith, Robert Cassidy, Roy and Alice Brown, Bruce and Rosalie Thomas, Jody and Susan Smith, Fred and Debbie Sutton, Dave and Triana Burrill, Mark and Mary Johnson, Larry and Janet Doolen, Karl and Linda Magnuson, John and Janet Everett, Dan and Gwen Centa, Howard and Carla Copeland, Ralph and Faye Wienbrooer, Ken and Shirley Deal, Hal and Joyce Clem,Tom and Diane Seaman,, Brad and Lori Pepper, Glen and Donna Steelman, Mark and Trudy Hewitt, Bob and Gwen Kuntz, Bob and Sherry Carter, Dan and Linda Siek, Gary and Jean Goodman, Dan and Elaine Rogers, Patrick and Cheryl Rogers,Tom and Geri Rose, Keith and Celinda Olszewski, Larry and Yvonne Alan, John and Linda Duguid, Steve and Vee Stanley, Tom and Maxine Logan, Bill and Erna Kirkoff, Dan and Evelyn Rodgers,Roy Brown, Doug and Gerry Gifford, Larry and Becky Lawhead, Cecil and Tippi Charles, Dr Dave and Dee Claassen, Dr Glen and Mary Lou Hultgren, Gary and Joyce Goulet, Ken and Maddy Dragoo, Frank and Diane Shinnick, Harlan and Marlene Seibel, Harry and Wanda Torres, Mark and Ann English, Patrick and Donna Schlachter, Rick and Pam Sanchez, Ted and Katie Crowell, Will and Trish Grubbs, Art Mitsutome, Lonnie and Trish Willis, Marvin and Millie Bay, John and Jane Everitt, Jerry and Rebekah Harrell, Gil and Jean Johnson, Harlan and Marlene Seibel, Jeremiah and Carole Way.

To my beloved brothers and sisters in Ukraine (Yuri, Gennady, Natasha, Alona, Shasha, and Igor) with the Gideon ministry, God bless you all--Slava Bogu. You will always be in my heart.

Friends in Rwanda

To beloved Papa Jo and Mama Grace and all the champions at the Home of Champions in Rwanda, and also to Paul and Jenn Woods who were precious friends to Isaac and Serena, with Henry during those precious years serving in Africa. Salute to Third Day Victory Church for their steadfast support.

Surely we will not know until heaven just how much others did for us in praying and helping and many times the most vital people in our life are overlooked.

Boulder men's group

Some of my best brother experiences have been at Second Street Baptist Church where I experienced wonderful fellowship in Jesus. You can feel the spirit of Jesus in this group - it is sweet and sincere.

Thank you Mick, Hal, Will, Wayne, Arnold, Gene, Carl, Roc, Doug, Randy, Vern, and so many special brothers. Peace in Jesus always.

Thank you Lord.

16. Love lasts forever ... Honeymoons

"Live happily with the woman you love" Ecclesiastes 9:9

God blesses with wonderful Honeymoons

You have to be kidding

As Donna and I approached our twenty-fifth wedding anniversary, I was looking at a Colorado map from our home in Minnesota and found a little town of Ouray in the southwest corner of the state. I called the Best Western to see if they had a room for the week of July 4.

The lady at the front desk answered and when she heard my request, she said, "You have to be kidding."

No, I was not kidding.

She went on to say, "People make reservations in Ouray a year or two in advance--especially on July 4 week."

I immediately knew I was not "with it."

Then she said, "Excuse me please," and I went on hold. After a while, she came back on the phone and said, "I just had a cancellation for the week of July 4. Would you like the room?"

"Yes, please."

So, off we went, Donna Kay and I headed for Ouray, Colorado in 1989 on the July 4 week. We were privileged to drop Kyle and Serena with Cherri and Rich in Rifle, Colorado where they lived and commuted to Glenwood Springs for work. While Donna Kay and I celebrated time in Ouray, Rich and Cherri entertained Kyle and Serena—they had a blast and we had a blast.

Donna and I discovered the spectacular scenery, hiking, jeeping, good food, and especially the community hot springs pool where we could shower, soak, and swim while looking at the mountains that surround us. Ouray is one of the few towns that still feels like a mountain town, relaxed and not overrun with yuppies.

We took the Silverton Narrow Gauge train ride out of Durango. We took an option of meeting the bus early in Silverton, riding down to the train in a bus, then taking the train back to Silverton. From there, we were able to go back to Ouray and relax in our own cabin.

Donna and I love to take time to read through the scriptures each year, a short prescribed reading each day. It is not a burden, but a delight. During that week, and ever since, we delighted in two passages we came cross in the book of Job.

I always share with people that reading through the Bible is like going through the mountains. You see familiar places and you never get weary of seeing them. They always have a little different light and hue—insight for living.

In Job 26, God talks about all the glories of His creation. We sure witnessed these glories in the mountains, including the thunderstorms that rumbled through and echoed back and forth in the spectacular high-altitude canyons, or the mountain streams and waterfalls that crashed off the mountainsides, and the magnificent splashes of mountain flowers, all colors and varieties.

God is awesome. God is mighty.

We always enjoyed some of our favorite jeep trails: Engineer, Cinnamon, Hurricane, Corkscrew, Ophir, California, Imogene, Last Dollar Road, and then a favorite out of Ridgeway.

> *Job 26;14 comments on all the glorious creation of God .. "These are merely a whisper of His power, who can understand the thunder of His power. " In NKJ, He says, "This is just the fringe".*
>
> *Wow. We are always so overwhelmed with His beauty, but is all just the edge of all he has to show us. Praise God.*

In Job 28, God talks about how men go into the earth and look for gold and silver, and that is exactly how the west was explored and settled. To this day, there is still some independent searches for gold and silver in Colorado, and there are a few full-size mines operating.

We were reading a book of mountain men stories and all the things they did to find gold. One story told of a man who decided to stay the winter in his cabin and was found frozen in the spring. Then there was the one about the mountain man who was delivering the mail from Fairplay to Leadville across Mosquito Pass and got caught in a blizzard on a fall day and died.

As God talks about these people searching for gems and jewels and minerals of value, he stops in Job 28:12-28:

> *"But do people know where to find wisdom? Where can they find understanding? No one knows where to find it for it is not found among the living. It is not here says the ocean, not here, says the sea. It cannot be bought for gold or silver! Its value is greater than all the gold of Ophir, greater than precious onyx stone or sapphires. Wisdom is far more valuable than gold or crystal. It cannot be purchased with jewels mounted in gold. Coral and valuable rock crystal are worthless in trying to get it. The price of wisdom is above pearls "*

By the way, Ophir Pass out of Ouray is a spectacular drive which we traveled many times. On one trip, we met John Davis, a pilot from Estes Park, who was a mutual Gideon. I had talked with him on the phone but never met him in person. I did that day. That was a nugget for the day.

God is good.

You can rent a jeep for the day and have the time of your life–don't forget to take along maps, sunglasses, sunscreen, water, and snacks.

God has just done a really fine job in Ouray of displaying the beauties of His creation.

He goes on to tell how He set the universe in order and created laws of God and then continues in Job 28:27-28:

> *"Then, when He had done all this, He saw wisdom and measured it. He established it and examined it thoroughly. And is what He says to all humanity. The fear of the Lord is true wisdom; to forsake evil is real understanding.".*

Not easy to take annual "honeymoons"

It is not easy to take honeymoons while you have small children. It is hard to have enough money, and it can be difficult to find someone willing and able to watch the children.

As a result, Donna Kay and I weren't always able to have a long anniversary celebration. We did something special each year, but sometimes it was a simple picnic, a sightseeing trip, or a weekend camping trip. Several times we went to the mountains for the night, and other times we got away for three or four days.

No matter how long or short, or what we did, it was the time to celebrate the years behind and the years before us.

We encourage other couples to take the time to honor each other and your marriage. A a couple times we got away, and Donna worried about the children. But after a few days, her dedication to the children was replaced by the pleasure of being away, and I was the one who had to remind her "we must go back, sweetheart".

What is it ? A cruise to Alaska?

Donna and I were approaching our thirty-fifth anniversary year, and I was again trying to find something special for us to do. Meanwhile, Betty Coble mentioned a special trip and special deal for a cruise to Alaska, so I thought I would surprise Donna.

Coming home one day in February from my real estate business, I said, "I got you a special gift today for your birthday and our annual honeymoon."

Donna said, "What is it? A cruise to Alaska?"

That took the wind out of my surprise sails, let me tell you. What can I say? She can read my mind. She knows all about everything.

Then she said, “What time of year are we going?”

So, I told her early June, and then she immediately knew–not only did she know what the gift was, but she knew I made a mistake in the timing.

It would probably be rainy.

After 35 years of marriage, I still struggle with humbling myself, with listening to my wife's advice, and with involving her in important decision.

Despite the weather, God was with us and blessed us and helped us enjoy our time together.

The trip consisted of eight-day cruise from Vancouver, BC to Seward, Alaska and then another four-day trip on a train from Anchorage to Fairbanks, and then a flight home. It was great, and having everything laid out made it relaxing and so off we went.

We had never been on a cruise. Donna was right, it was a little chilly, especially when on the ocean. We purchased new jackets to keep us warm and dry.

There were a few special things we saw along the way:

Ketchikan was a fishing village. Although the day was overcast, we went into town to get the idea of what a true fishing town looked like. We had lunch at a local diner, and the clam chowder was good. We also went to the local Goodwill or Habitat store and browsed their offerings. After a cold and damp day on shore, it was good to get back to our cozy room on the ship, which was excellent.

Skagway was the popular entry point to the gold rush in the Yukon, so we got off the ship for a train ride that took us to the top of the ridge that overlooked the trail to the goldfields as the engineer told stories of the old miners and their exploits.

We also stopped at Juneau, the capitol. This is a spectacular place nestled beside Admiralty Bay. We took a boat ride out to see the whales, the eagles, and the glaciers coming from the north. We then took a hike and saw a bear. Bears and eagles and whales are in abundance. Finally, we took a tram to the top of the mountain where we could see out over the region. It was a beautiful place.

Walt and Roberta from Loveland were with us, along with Betty Coble and her husband. We met for dinner a couple times and enjoyed their friendship.

Glacier Bay National Park

We asked God to help us find a Christian couple that we could fellowship with on the cruise. God answered that prayer, and we met a nice Christian couple who liked to play cards. So, we met at 2:00 p.m. each day and had a social time. Of course, we had all the food and drink we needed or wanted anytime. We also enjoyed walking on the walking deck, usually on the seventh floor.

I went to the purser and asked if someone had planned a church service on Sunday morning.

"Don't think so" said the purser. "We have not heard from any pastors on the boat."

"Well, here is my name and room number in case someone decides to do a service. They could ask me to help."

Now I am not a formal pastor but I had spent 30 years in a church function as both preacher and worship leader, and I was comfortable doing anything.

On Saturday night at 9:30 p.m., the ship newsletter was slipped under our door. We read it to see what was happening the next day, and a small note caught our eye: "a volunteer on the ship has agreed to do a church service on Sunday morning at 8:00 a.m. at the lounge area".

I said to Donna, "Do you suppose that is me?"

Sunday morning, we went to breakfast and went down to the lounge area at about 7:30 a.m., and two young men greeted us.

One of the men says, “I will be doing the sound for you.”

The other man, Ben from London, said, “I will be playing the piano.“

Because he wasn’t a Christian, he was not sure if he knew the songs in the hymnbook but said he would give it a whirl.

This was going to be interesting.

I gave them each a Gideon testament and witnessed to them. I had brought 50 to give out, and did so, coming back home with zero.

I glanced over and saw a stack of songbooks. I was delighted. I also noticed a couple ladies down front and thought, this may be small but we will go with it. By the time 8:00 a.m. came, the room was filled to more than 100 folk.

I was pleasantly surprised.

I got up and explained I was a volunteer and welcomed them. I said, “We will open with prayer and then sing requests for songs, and then later we will open the mic for anyone wanting to share.”

We had a wonderful time of singing, and Ben did quite well on the piano. Donna was right there on the front row helping me sing. She was such an encouragement to me.

When I stopped leading songs to allow an “open mic” time, a gentleman from New York, who I had met in the gym, came forward with his Bible in hand and shared a wonderful message of the gospel of Jesus.

Perfect.

As the hour came to 9:00 a.m., I thanked all for coming and thanked the two young men who helped, and I mentioned if someone had a song they missed singing to come on down, and Donna and I would sing with them.

One gentleman came down to see Jerry and said, “Let me guess, you are a Gideon.”

God is so good.

The next special sight was the Glacier Bay National Park where the ship moves very slowly because there are pieces of ice in the huge bay with mountains and glaciers all around. The sight of seeing glaciers “calf”—when big chucks of ice break off and go into the water—was amazing, and again we saw a grizzly on the beach moving about.

When we got to land at Seward, we were taken on a bus to Anchorage and had a wonderful night eating at a pizza place in Anchorage on Donna Kay's birthday. The next day we got on the train.

The train ride was very pleasant. The U.S. Government, who bought the railroad from the original owners in the early 1900's, gave Alaska the train and rail system in 1985. The State of Alaska remodeled the trains and stations, and has maintained the system ever since.

The dome cars allowed us to see outside, and two young tour guides were lots of fun, sharing as appropriate on the way. The days remained overcast and we could not see a full view of Mount McKinley, but we saw enough to marvel at God's creative hand.

We were amazed at the stories of how the railroad was built in this inclement land. In some places, the areas were so swampy that much of the work must wait until winter when the ground is frozen and workers can use snowmobiles to move about.

One unique custom which we found endearing was that the train would stop for anyone along the train rails. Because this is deep wilderness, and folks take care of each other, the people who live and visit there know not to take advantage of this practice

We heard about the northern lights in the winter and the cold. The girl tour guide shared how folks sit in a hot tub on a winter night and put water on their hair and lift it up and it would immediately freeze, and they could break it off like ice.

The next stop was Denali National Park. The park workers work very hard to keep this park pristine. There is only 50 miles of road and only the buses go in. In the winter, only sled dogs are allowed—no snowmobiles. The sled dogs were amazing to watch. The handlers brought out six dogs and harnessed them to the sled. We could tell by their broad chests and powerful haunches that they were very powerful.

The lead dog is the smart and obedient one that the master can trust. The wheel dogs are very strong and make sure that the master is protected. So, as they went in and around the trees turning here and there, those dogs made sure that the sled never hit anything.

As we took the trip on the bus into the park, we saw Dahl sheep on the mountains, caribou, grizzly bear, and moose. The driver and tour guide told us that since Denali is so far north, the oxygen levels are lower, which is why the trees are small and the number of wildlife is limited.

There is a clear sense in Alaska of its vastness. In fact, if you really want to go anywhere very far, you need a plane. Most everyone flies—that is, they use airplanes.

When the bus came to the end of the tour, we were treated to hot chocolate and a time to stretch outside the bus. However, they gave firm warning to not drop anything. Even a drop of hot chocolate on the ground would attract wild animals, especially grizzlies, and they don't want the creatures to get familiar with human foods.

From Denali, the train took us to Fairbanks. I thought it would be boring because we were headed for the coast. However, the ride turned out to be a surprise. We enjoyed a riverboat ride, another tour of the huskies, and listening to stories about the dogs.

We stopped in to see Susan Butcher and her husband who lived along the river. They had many dogs. She had won the Iditarod race—a long 1,000-mile grueling trek across the winter tundra with their dogs.

Susan told a story of a race where all of a sudden, the dogs tried to go off the trail. She jerked them back. They tried again, and this time she let them go their way.

They pulled her off the trail and up on a ridge. She stopped. Then she heard the cracking of the ice on the lake they just left.

That was a close call. She never doubted her dogs again.

God was good to Donna and me. It was a wonderful honeymoon.

Renew the fire

Renewing the fire of your love for each other is so vital. We try to have a weekly date, and we try to make sure we have a good visit each day to maintain a warm and loving relationship. We have found that a longer time together once a year gives us time to talk about our plans for the future, to encourage and edify each other in our spiritual journey, and to reconnect on a deeper and more intimate level than a day or weekend provides.

To give each other undivided attention for a time is very important, and to also build wonderful memories, is critical to the longevity of any marriage. Time spent together is like driving a stake in the ground again of your commitment and companionship for life.

Nothing is more important than God and your mate. We do not have the promise of many years, so enjoy each year, each day. Here are a few more memories.

Brown County, Indiana

When Donna and I lived in Green Castle, Indiana, we were blessed to have Ray and Donna, my parents, visit and watch the kids while Donna and I went to Brown County for a get-away. Since our anniversary is in the fall, it was beautiful in Brown County. We stayed in a warm and clean cabin, and took hikes and enjoyed a relaxing few days. We went to Story, Indiana for dinner one night and also visited a local art studio.

North shore of Minnesota

We don't quite remember who stayed with the kids, but it was probably Dave and Linda Mosbo. So, off we went to the north shore of Minnesota right at the end of September and first of October. We stayed in a lodge south of Canadian border.

As we sat down for dinner that night, we noticed that hardly anyone was there.

Duh.

We were one of the last people to stay during that season.

While we were there, it started to snow. It was lovely and it meant we were more inclined to stay in our cabin. You're never too old to find things to occupy your time when you are with your honey.

From there, we went down to Duluth where we stayed at a bed and breakfast owned by a doctor and his wife. The house was built to imitate a quaint old castle. We went to bed and not long after, heard someone trying to get into the room.

Donna woke me. "Jerry, somebody is rattling the doorknob."

I wasn't quite awake, so I called out, "Who's there?"

When there was no answer, we went back to sleep and thought no more of it.

The next morning, when we came down for breakfast, I looked at the person that seemed to be in charge and said, "Were one of you trying to open our door last night?"

The lady said apologetically, "I was just checking the doors to make sure they were locked, and did not know you were in there. We actually show tours of this place when people are not here. Sorry."

We all laughed, because if we hadn't locked the door, their tour would have had a sight more than they were expecting.

Then we enjoyed a hardy breakfast.

Crested Butte area

This is one of our favorite spots as you leave Crested Butte on Slate Road to Paradise Divide

I made arrangements to rent a condo in the Crested Butte ski area the July 4 weekend. We enjoyed day trips and discovered Paradise Divide up Slate Creek, Washington Gulch, Gothic, and Schofield Pass. What a beautiful area.

Locals claim Crested Butte is the wildflower capitol of Colorado. We found a place on the mountainside to watch the fireworks, and were able to make a very simple exit to our condo after the fireworks instead of having to go through tons of traffic had we been back home.

We discovered a terrific surprise off a trail on Washington Gulch. It was a beautiful wooden set of chairs with a small table attached between. It had been shellacked several times and had a brass plate stating it was "Dedicated to our father", and another plate saying, "Approved by National Forest."

It was perfect for us to sit down, rest, eat our lunch, and read a book while looking down the at the beautiful valley scenery. God's creation is fantastic back there. This has become a repeatable area for our enjoying.

Recently we went up to Lake Irwin near Crested Butte to spend some time with Shelby and Lora and their precious family as they provide service as a host during the summer. This is a gorgeous place. We are so proud of them for their good work there.

Thirteen passes

God bless Donna for putting up with this guy.

I had planned a trip in Sam, the little red ragtop jeep. Sam could go anywhere, maybe a little small, but we felt very safe. Sam was equipped with a manual transmission and it was fun to be in the open with rag top.

We were packed and ready to go. It was an night in early September with a full moon. I got up at 12:30 a.m. after getting a couple hours of sleep and asked Donna if we could go.

She shook her head to clear out the cobwebs, and off we went. Going over Trail Ridge at 2:00 a.m. and seeing the elk in the moonlight was a lot of fun.

As the day went on, we went across Hoosier Pass and down to Buena Vista and up over Cottonwood Pass and Cumberland Pass. At about 3:30 p.m., we found a place along the river to camp, had some dinner, and went to bed. It rained all night long, but we were safe and dry. God took care of us.

Of course, we ended up in Ouray for a few days. In the process of getting to Ouray and getting back home over the next few days, we went across thirteen passes–miles of beautiful country.

Jerry & Donna continue to enjoy mountain days.
This is north of Pagosa Springs

Teton National Park

Another time, toward the end of the summer, we rented a popup tent, packed, and left real early and stopped somewhere in Wyoming just as the sun was rising. We got out and had communion together. Breakfast was in Lander, and we headed for the Teton National Park where we had reserved a campsite.

One day, we took a drive through Yellowstone, stopping at Fish Bridge with otters, buffalo, and eagles. From the road, we saw a bear climbing a tree. It didn't seem the least bit fazed by the long line of cars pulled off the road, the passengers clicking cameras at the sight.

Another day we rented a boat to go across Jackson Lake. The man who rented the boat told us it would be no problem to find our way. He said as we started across, we would come to one island and then another and another and pretty soon it seemed like finding our spot coming back would be a trick.

It was gorgeous. The water was perfectly clear. As we went north and started to come back south, an Air Force jet flew west toward the Tetons and then banked and came right at us and skimmed across the water as if he were putting on a show just for us on our honeymoon.

Donna is a terrific wife. She is willing to go along with whatever plans I come up with. She is flexible, and is always prepared whether we cook out, or stop at a restaurant or diner to eat, or eat out of the cooler. It was all fun. We also took our Bibles and other books to read, as well as several games, so we were never bored.

Rio Grande headwaters

Donna and I visited George and Carol Davis in Center, which is close to Alamosa. From there, we went in their Explorer to Creede and headed up the Rio Grande headwaters, which is a fifty-mile jeep road that exits down a steep pass called Stony into Silverton.

This was a great trip. We camped, not far from Creede, in a rustic place and then headed out the next day. We came to a pretty good- sized creek that we had to go through in the jeep. Fortunately, there was another jeep that had just crossed so we through with assurance.

There was a place several miles in, where we came through a small opening and saw a sign–Brewster Ranch–and then we went through a beautiful valley. We paused to survey the land, and I wished that either Phil Brewster, my good friend, or Larry Brewster, my brother-in-law, could see that place.

We came to an off-road trail to Bear City. So, off we went and we arrived at Bear City, which is little more than a few abandoned buildings with a cold lake nearby. In fact, the water was so cold, there was still a blanket of snow ringing it. A storm was coming, and it was getting real dark. Donna asked me to get back down off the mountain, so we did.

As we came close to Stony Pass, we could see south into the Weminuchee Wilderness. A sign indicated the option of a hike that appeared to be several miles to the edge of the pass. But because of the late hour, we went on down Stony Pass and found our way back to our favorite resting place, Ouray.

As these stories are told, we are reminded of how God always cared for us.

Utah and Zion National and Grand Canyon

On another trip, Donna and I headed down to Ridgeway and over into Utah where we camped. It was early fall and the leaves had turned. Then we went across Utah heading for Zion National Park where we had reservations at the lodge, recommended by friend Mel McCauley.

We enjoyed Escalante Canyon, but in general, we found Utah was too hot and too dry and not too inviting – yet pretty in its own way.

Zion National Park was beautiful, and we were glad we had brought our bicycles with us, carrying them on the back of the Explorer. There were no bike trails, but since only an occasional bus goes through there, it was safe to ride up the road. The food and the wildlife was grand and it was wonderfully quiet.

The hike we took was very special, ending with a final scramble to "Angel Point" on a ledge path that we chose not to take. Besides, we see angel points all the time with their angels. Praise God.

We went from Zion to the north rim of the Grand Canyon. That year, the park experienced fires down in the canyon. It was smoky so we did not stay long. We went to the campground which was full and so we couldn't stay. The attendant said, "Go out the road, and as you come to CR 611, you will find a nice rustic campsites along the canyon."

We following his instructions and found the place, which had some vacancies. We had a wonderful time.

Jerry and Donna together and happy in the Lord.

As we traveled across Arizona, we stopped at Monument Valley. The Navajo Nation operates that area, overseeing its maintenance. John Wayne filmed several movies here, and the goal is to leave the area as it was during the filming of these movies. It was beautiful.

As we headed back toward Colorful Colorado, we came to a little town named Bluff, Utah. It was quiet, small, and had a trading post filled with Navajo blankets, jewelry, and many quality products that we enjoyed. Then, coming back into Colorado through Cortez and Telluride, we realized how beautiful and colorful Colorado is—teeming with rivers and water, and so much greener as compared to the dry places in Arizona and Utah.

Poudre Valley Cabin

One year, I reserved a cabin up the Poudre River for us on our anniversary week, the first part of September. Meanwhile, my father called and said that one of his siblings had died and the funeral was the same time we had reserved the cabin.

I told Dad I would be there for the funeral, then called to change the cabin reservation. The soonest date we could book was the first week of October.

When we arrived at the cabin, it was very nice, but the fall leaves were already on the ground, and the weather was cold. The fireplace came in handy, and we got out for day trips up into the mountains.

Paonia house for a week

Precious friends have a house in Paonia that sits empty except when they go over in September to pick peaches. Earl and Jenetta always said, "Stop and use the house."

So, we finally took them up on their offer.

The town of Paonia is small and quiet, and we found a little church and visited on Sunday morning. Each day, we took a day trip, either hiking or driving. We explored Crawford south and down onto the Blue Mesa and back over Ohio Pass. We discovered Lake Irwin where Shelby and Lora camp every year when they come up from Texas.

We met a Doctor Wright and his wife who wanted to retire from busy Denver, and found the quiet town of Paonia. They invited us over for dinner. They bought an older home, built by a retired Navy Admiral. This beautiful house has seventy windows. The Wrights also did quite a bit of remodeling, including installing gorgeous marble over the fireplace with the words "Think about eternity" engraved in the stone.

Westcliff Cabin

For another anniversary, we rented a cabin outside Westcliff on the Sangre De Cristo range, and we arrived on a Monday. It was late in the season, and the owner said we would find the key in the cabin and that everyone else would be gone.

So, we picked up the key and got our bags inside. Donna was fixing dinner, and we went out on the deck while it was cooking.

Someone—and we're not pointing fingers here—pulled the door shut. Pure habit.

The only problem was, it was locked.

And the key was inside.

I was able to remove the front screen and go retrieve the key.

Another adventure. Another memory.

The Sangre De Cristo range is very rugged. We drove the jeep down a long trail to a trailhead then hiked to a beautiful lake. We like the town of Westcliff. It reminded us of the towns in old westerns which were welcoming with zero commercial development.

The ranchers in that area have done well to keep their ranches, not selling off their land for development. It is a beautiful area in the state.

Jerry and Donna taking time to enjoy God's creation

Elk Run Cabin

One year we wanted to go to Ouray.

At least, I did.

But August was packed with activities and no time, and then September was packed with activities and no time, so I got on the website and found a "for rent by owner" cabin.

I called, and sure enough, the first week of October was open. This place was up the mountain about seven miles, and it was a cabin owned by a doctor and his family from Indiana. Boy, did we enjoy staying up there.

The weather turned out perfect with gorgeous fall weather, changing of leaves, and good walking days. Of course, we got down to the pool in Ouray. One of our favorite drives is out on CR 5 outside Ridgeway where you drive back into a picture-perfect place.

We took some day trips and were able to find out about the beautiful gated area where we were staying. We called the place where we rented the "bear house" because in early fall, many bears hang around there for the berry bushes.

Kyle and Margie came with Ruby, and we had a great time. We enjoyed the fall colors and glorious setting with God.

That night, the snowstorm came in. During the night, I woke up and there were no lights–no electricity. I got up, lit candles, and started a good fire. Kyle and Margie got up with Donna and me. We talked a while around the fire and then went back to bed.

In the morning, the lights were on and all was okay.

A favorite stop on the way home is the apple warehouse in Delta where we get a box or two of apples for applesauce makings. Yum.

50th Honeymoon to the Northeast

God blessed us with the time and the resources to take a month off for our 50th anniversary. The financial resources were provided by Kelli Couch, my business partner in Real Estate, and I got the time off from my good boss Kevin LeMasters.

We started out on October 1 and headed to Kansas where we spent time with Donna's sweet sister Betty Keeler and met family from the Smith side: David and Kim Gustafson, Glenda and Charlie, Richard and Alvin Newell, Alberta Milton from St John, Shawn and Sherri with Parker and little grandson .

From left ; Dave Gustafson, Betty Keeler, Kim Gustafson, Shawn Smith behind,Donna Kay and Jerry, Sherry Smith, and Parker.

On October 6, we visited our good friends, Darrell and Donna Castor in Verona, Missouri. They live in a beautiful home in the country and have a pond and horses, We had a great visit. Darrell and Donna came to Colorado a couple years ago and helped us to distribute 40,000 scriptures. They are dear friends.

Darrell and Donna Caster in Verona, Mo

Bill and Jennifer Moran in Kentucky

Cousin Tom Schick, Phyllis, Dee, and Greg in Columbus, Ohio

Niagara Falls was worth the trip and New York upstate is beautiful.

We then went to Maine, crossing Vermont and New Hampshire. All along the way, our GPS was a life saver to lead us to Old Orchard and a wonderful room looking over the ocean. We could hear the waves and go down to walk on the beach. .

"May the glory of the Lord last forever! He rejoices in all He has made!" Psalms. 104:31

This was the view from our "penthouse" room in Maine.

We enjoyed going to Acadia National Park and going up Cadillac Mountain that overlooks the ocean and many islands. Many people visit this park to enjoy the hiking, the bike paths, and the diversity of the scenery.

We also spent a night in Ellsworth with Ann Bancroft and her husband. We found them through the Mennonite Way Book. From there we left very early and drove all the way to our B&B in Rutland, Vermont.

Jerry and Donna having lunch in Bar Harbor Maine.

Ken and Lisa, from Mississippi, were guests with us at a B&B in Vermont. .

Mike and Barb Young top picture were our B&B hosts, and Will and Sarah were guests from England

Covered bridge near Rutland, Vermont

A favorite visit to Woodstock, Vermont .

As we travelled, we enjoyed time with God each morning in our daily walk in Word and Spirit and prayer for our family, friends, and Gideon prayer list. We focused on a different "love dare" each week. Week 1 was patience, week 2 kindness, week 3 thoughtfulness, week 4 unselfishness, and week 5 was not being rude. We also shared 10/10 from time to time while we ate together. We read a book on the Orphan Spirit, which is one of satan's schemes, versus being a victorious child of God, which is, of course, God's plan. We also read a good biography of Laura Bush.

Waterfalls, rivers, hills, and trees abounded along with the trees. We took it one day at a time for over 7,000 miles. God blessed us with a wonderful Volvo that got excellent mileage, and gas prices were exceptional. We would get out and walk in the woods. We are so thankful for all who prayed for us as we went.

From Rutland we headed to Owego, New York where our good friends Bill and Sue Anderson kept us for three days over the weekend. I had invited Bill to church while we lived in Greeley in late 60's, which is where Bill met Sue. Bill and Sue now live in southern New York with the Finger Lakes and its waterfalls. The area is lush and beautiful. Bill and Sue lead a wonderful church in Owego.

Home of Bill and Sue Anderson in Owego, New York

We saw an apple outlet, and we watched apple cider being made. Thank you, Bill and Sue, for sharing your love of the area with us.

The cabin above is their home in the country.

The buggies of the Amish as we visited Walnut Creek, Ohio area. This ride was a gift from Phil and Emily Esau.

A creative fall display below with classic pickup .

One of the back roads among the Amish farms. Praise God for their industrious ways that keep roads and farms very neat.

Glory be to God for the precious Amish who live in humble dedication to God. Everything is peaceful and beautiful, and they truly set an example of industry and integrity in a world that is so very different.

We spent three days visiting my dear cousin Phil and we stayed with Emily and Charlie the dog. We had a wonderful stay there in Dayton Ohio, even sang in their choir. This is their lovely home, and our rented Volvo. Phil was in the hospital while we were there, so we continued to pray for his feet to heal and for him to be restored.

Home of Phil and Emily Esau.

Emily walking Charley and Donna Kay right behind .

Ken and Lee Baxter precious friends in Lexington, Ky. Such precious friends, gentle and kind.

One of the beautiful farms in Lexington, Ky

We moved on from there to Nashville, Tennesee to visit with Jesse and Jane Gough, what precious friends living in a perfectly-decorated home with love abounding. We had a great visit and ate at their favorite restaurant with an exceptional salad and soup meal.

Then we headed out for Van Buren, Arkansas leaving at 4:30 a.m. and arriving at 4:30 p.m. Wow, Seemed it always took longer to get there than GPS showed. Maybe that had something to do with the number of stops we enjoyed along the way.

We stayed with Elliott and Sherry Hays. Elliott and I were in Ukraine together with the Gideon distribution of 110,000 scriptures, We had a great fellowship as we attended church with them after Elliott and I attended the 7:00 am Gideon prayer time.

Dr. Elliott took us to his office later that evening, did a quick test, and was able to coach us on our things we could do to become healthier. Certainly his laughter was good for our health.

Proverbs 17:22 "A cheerful heart is like good medicine, but a broken spirit saps a person's strength".

Picture in Elliott home Judge Parker 'hanging judge gallows'

There is always laughter with Dr Elliott. Thank you for all your good advice, friend. We really like Arkansas with lots of trees and lakes and down home folk. His "son" is Backery who does ministry for Jesus.

Home of Karen and Jim Crain in Oklahoma City with Kenny Keeler, Christy and family, Mike and Katie, and Brody and Katie and all their children.

Another early morning as we left Jim and Karen's home, we had a little scare. Their neighborhood has a gate which was closed. Since it was 4:00 a.m., we did not want to disturb anybody, but as we tried to open the gate, the alarm went off. Security showed up and waved us on our way.

We enjoyed being in the prairies of Texas after seeing so many trees for so many days, marveling at the beauty.

But by now we'd come to realize that every state had its own kind of beauty.

We traveled through 16 states during our trip: Colorado, Kansas, Missouri, Illinois, Kentucky, Ohio, Pennsylvania, New York, Vermont, New Hampshire, Maine, Tennessee, Arkansas, Oklahoma, Texas, and New Mexico . We stayed 19 nights in the homes of gracious hosts and 9 nights in BB or motels, and we slept well each night.

Thanks again for hospitality to Betty Keeler, Darrell and Donna Castor, Jennifer and Bill Moran, Tom and Carol Schick, Ann Bancroft, Mike and Barb Young, Bill and Sue Anderson, Phil and Emily Esau, Ken and Lee Baxter, Jesse and Jane Gough, Elliott and Sherry Hays, Jim and Karen Crane, and Kyle and Margie Swanson.

In Amarillo Texas having breakfast, Donna with waitress, Lisa who gladly prayed with us

All across the country, we asked our waitress how we might pray for them as they served us, and we got some rather passive responses and some sincere replies. In good ol' Texas, we asked Lisa how we could pray for her. She reached out her hands and said, "let's pray".

"anyone who fears the Lord is my friend" Psalms 119:63

We were trying to reach Taos, New Mexico at the end of a 600-mile day. We went up to the high mountain lodge at Angel Fire and were treated royally. We then drove down the next day to Eagles Nest and Red River and then took Kyle's advice to see Wild River.

This is the end of the San De Christo mountains coming back into Colorado after a month trip

After a month away, it was absolutely glorious to see the snow-capped mountains again, north of the State line after leaving Taos area. We were able to head for Kyle and Margie's for a night before getting home. God bless them!

17. God helps and God Refines and Re-Fires.

"So humble yourselves under the mighty power of God and in His good time He will honor you ...Give all your cares to God, for He cares about what happens to you. After you have suffered awhile, he will restore, support, and strengthen you, and He will place you on a firm foundation "1 Peter 5:6,10

While we lived in Seattle, we attended Bill Gothard Basic Youth Conflicts seminars, and he and his staff have printed up the most beautiful books called Character Sketches. They are quality books with a character theme, with stories from the Bible, and also stories of animals that reflect characters.

Another group that teaches character is Character First. They provide all kinds of materials on character building. Of course, the Bible is the best source of character building with stories of men and women who lived honorably and those who made mistakes.

It is wise to learn from others' mistakes and not make our own.

Well, we do not seem to be astonished that over the years of our life things have changed. It used to be the father worked outside the home and was the head of the home and spiritual leader, while the mother is the homemaker, cares for the home, and makes it a place of refuge and health where God is welcome.

All this is now very rare. Our culture has grown more and more godless, and more and more against the Christian family. Today the Christian home is pulled in many directions.

God keeps refining us, and one of the phrases of Bill Gothard says is, "Please be patient with me, God is not finished with me yet." Another phrase was "God does not make junk." God is working on us and He is patient to get the job done.

For fifty years of marriage, God has been working to refine us as we have been seeking Him and finding wisdom from His Word. We have learned little by little. One of the inspirations in our life are the godly people that surround us. In Hebrews 12, the scripture reminds us to "Seeing a great cloud of witnesses, run the race with patience, keeping your eyes on Jesus".

One of the areas of refinement for me was being wise with money. Wanting to help others and live a good and generous life, I was quick to borrow money, and quick to lend to some who could not or would not replay. Debt is a very dangerous habit.

While running hard to serve and minister and help, I welcomed offers for borrowed money and debts mounted. I was sure I could pay them off, until business and income stopped, and I could not pay those debts.

We lost everything we had, including our home, our car, and our business. That was a hard time for us as we sought the help of God. After five years of seeking His help and the help of others, we have been refined and are doing much better. Gradually we have been able to pay off our debts and are still doing it. It was not wise.

However, I am still learning after fifty years to live within a budget and heed the good advice from Donna. There were times when we did not have gas for the car, but many people have worse problems, and God always provided in some way.

We may not have much money, but I consider myself to be the richest man in the world because I have a clear conscience with God and with man. I am blessed with a wonderful, godly wife and exceptional adult children who, in turn, have incredible children (our grandchildren). They are beautiful godly granddaughters and handsome godly grandsons.

Jerry and Donna stand together with the Lord

One of my favorite instructions from scripture was restated by my friend Brad Tuttle. Amos 3:3 says: “Can two people walk together without agreeing on the direction?” We now agree on what we spend. I heed Donna’s advice, and we stay together on God’s path.

One of the things that is so important is a willingness to communicate and pray together with humility, to share openly and not hide things, but to speak straight. It is not always easy. And while it may e difficult to see from the outside looking in, we have a clear conscience before God and man.

We thank God that He is the God of second chances.

Following Jesus is not easy. One day, my men's group was going to be reading and discussing 1 Peter 4.

I jokingly said to Bob Tholl the leader, "I do not want to participate because this chapter is about suffering and I do not need that now."

However, after the study, I was glad I went. It was good to note that the scripture says, "Jesus will suffer with you." It is good to know that our God does not desert us when we are in the wilderness.

The disciples of Jesus lived with him for three years, and during that time, they were continually being refined. Refinement comes as we raise children and as we each take responsibilities at church, ministry, community, and business. It is humbling to be subject to many people. I have spent sleepless nights and more time on my knees depending on God.

In one job situation early in my IBM career, for seven years I was under incredible pressure and could never quite please the boss. I wanted to quit but did not, and looking back it seems like seven minutes instead of years. One of my most comforting verses is 1 Samuel 30:8 where David is ready to be stoned and the scripture says, "David encouraged himself in the Lord... do not quit, find strength in the Lord." Be patient with your path.

When things are not going well, it is good to share your burdens, and welcome prayers and advice. You may not take it, but at least listen and learn. Read, pray, and stay low.

Marriage is perhaps the best place to be learn how to be humble, to pray for each other, to bear each other's burdens, to learn together, and to praise God together as He brings you through tough times.

One of the themes God has brought into my life has been LBL or "little by little." In Deuteronomy, God gives instructions to His people to take the land little by little. God is a God of patience. He is not in a hurry. He is working out His plans for you. His plans are good.

During my years of leadership in The Gideons International as State President, I felt overwhelmed and helpless. One of the stories that God revealed to me is the story of Jehoshaphat in 2 Chronicles 20:

Many armies had gathered against Jehoshaphat and God's people. It was overwhelming. So he prays to God "O our God, won't you stop them? We are powerless against this mighty army that is about to attack. us. We do not know what to do, but we are looking to you for help."

> *"Then the Spirit of the Lord came upon one of them standing there named Jahaziel and he spoke God's message to Jehoshaphat "Listen, King Jehoshaphat ! Listen, all you people of Judah and Jerusalem! This is what the Lord says: Do not be afraid! Don't be discouraged by this mighty army, for the battles is not yours, but God's. Tomorrow, march out against them. You will find them coming up from the valley that opens into the wilderness of Jeruel. But you will not even need to fight. Take your positions; then stand still and watch the Lord's victory. He is with you. Do not be afraid or discouraged. Go out there tomorrow and the Lord is with you.*
>
> *Then Jehoshaphat bowed down with his face to the ground, and all the people of Judah and Jerusalem did the same, worshiping the Lord. Then the Levites from the clans of Kohath and Korah stood to praise the Lord, the God of Isreal, with a very loud shout."*
>
> *Early the next day, they went into the wilderness and Jehoshaphat stopped and said to the people "Believe in the Your God, and you will be able to stand firm. Believe in the prophets and you will prosper." Then the appointed singers walked ahead of the army singing to the Lord and praising Him for His holy splendor." So we go in faith to sing to the Lord and praise Him. Believe in God and watch. God will bless. Amen. 2 Chronicles 20.*

Our chance to escape

There was a movie called "Electric Horseman" where Robert Redford gets on his horse and heads west and escapes the chaos of his life. I have told people over the years if they do not see me, then that is what I did.

There have been times in my life when I wanted to just go to the mountains and be a recluse. When Donna and I dated in college, I wrote her love notes and talked about living together some day in a mountain cabin where it is quiet and no one to bother us.

So one day while my father was toward the end of his last career on the ranch he called me and offered me chance to escape. Of course, he did not say it that way. He simply said if I wanted to come to the ranch (it was actually the ranch of Wesley Wheeler in Waneta, Nebraska) then Dad would be willing to train me on what to do to be a good ranch hand.

Well, I wanted to do that with all my heart, but I had to tell my dad, no because I felt called to stay in the fray of life and reach people with the good news of Jesus, and escaping was not what God called me to do.

So I did not escape.

As a matter of fact, much of my life is spent standing right in the middle of a college campus, in the path of students coming and going, and offering them a free copy of the living Word of God so that they might know Jesus and have the wonderful life available in Him.

Re-fired by God

David had many trials in his life, and one of his deepest moments of despair was when his men were tired and hungry and worn and they came home to Gilgal to find their camp burning and their wives and children all captured (1 Samuel 30:1-5). It says the men sat down and wept until they could weep no more.

> *1 Samuel 30:6 "David was now in serious trouble because his men were very bitter about losing their wives and children, and they began to talk of stoning him. But David found strength in the Lord His God."*

This is the time when most people quit and give up on God.

There are times in a person's life when they are in very serious trouble and they just do not know what to do. At that time, we must turn to God for strength. David writes in Psalms 55:

> *"But I will call on God, and the Lord will rescue me. Morning, noon, and night I plead aloud in my distress, and the Lord hears my voice. He rescues me and keeps me safe from the battle waged against me, even though many oppose me."*

Make no mistake: life is hard. The enemy is out to destroy us. We look to God and Jesus for strength morning, noon, and night. And, we thank Him as he rescues us over and over.

So, after almost thirty years at IBM, I was able to retire. I was 52. I then looked for a second career that I found as a Realtor. That career lasted another 14 years and I retired again. This was not a smooth landing as I was working full-time in Gideon ministry and full-time in real estate. Most people think retirement is about sitting back and relaxing.

I spent some time praying with Donna and trying to figure out what we should do, and God woke me up at 3:00 a.m. one morning and said, "You are not retired but re-fired."

I knew what that meant. *Get back to what God wanted from me.* We sat down and wrote out 90-day goals and weekly goals. We still stay very focused and active in serving the Lord in ministries, and I work part- time for a great Christian company. We are also committed grandparents who help when we can, and we deeply love our grandchildren.

While others talk about another cruise or another round of golf, we choose to use our gifts to remain fruitful. God never said we sit on the bench just because we get older. We do our best to remain active.

One of the goals we have is to do more things together in ministry and with the family. We hope to help couples with being more successful in their marriage. We believe that a good marriage that is committed to walk together day by day with God will be a solid foundation for all the rest of their life. A strong marriage includes praying together and playing together every day.

Our home church is focusing on service to the community and neighbors this year. It is a great theme and clearly the Spirit of Christ, to serve. Those who learn how to serve others will be happy all the days of their life.

While writing this book, we spent time in a rural town in Nebraska named Hay Springs, and we met wonderful Christians who give their life to serving. It is refreshing to see.

As a matter of fact, these are life-long friends and we work to keep in touch with them: Rick and Loretta Roberts, Shirley Heiting, and also Marc and Judy Vahrenkamp who serve in the Gideon ministry. We were shown wonderful Christian hospitality and friendship while there, and we hope to visit again before too long.

Seeking God's wisdom for our lives is vital, and setting goals is powerful and refreshing as we look ahead to set a course of fruitful living. While life doesn't always work out as we want, it is better than just wandering along with no direction.

Paul Stanley of NavPress spoke at a men's retreat and shared the following challenge:

> *"Youth is not a period of time. It is a state of mind, a result of the will, a quality of the imagination, a victory of courage over timidity, the taste of adventure and over the love of comfort. A man doesn't grow old because he has lived a certain number of years, he grows old when he deserts his ideal. The years may wrinkle his skin, but deserting his ideal wrinkles his soul. Preoccupations, fear, doubts, and despair are the dust before death. You will remain young as long as you are open to what is beautiful, good and great; receptive to the messages of other men and women, of nature and of God. If one day you should become bitter, pessimistic and gnawed by despair, may God have mercy on your old man's soul." General Douglas MacArthur.*

I was privileged to have a father who set the pace. When my father retired from insurance at 62, he met Wes Wheeler, who is a wonderful Christian man of honor and rancher out of Wauneta, Nebraska. My father, Ray, asked Wes if he could use a hand. Wes said, "Five dollars an hour," and he could give it a try. Wes must have thought this greenhorn would not last a week.

After several weeks went by, Ray was doing fine. Wes asked, "Are you okay to ride a horse, since we need to round up the cows?"

Ray said, "I will try."

After that day, Wes said, "Ray, I think you have been holding out on me. "

Ray did not bother to tell Wes when he hired on that he had grown up ranching and riding. Ray worked 20 more years for Wes. No wonder he lived to be 92 before retiring in heaven.

So, we go on and look forward to days ahead as we find strength in God day-by-day to be refired and fruitful, and we continue to pray the promise of God in Psalms 92.

> *"Even in old age they will still produce fruit; they will remain vital and green. They will declare, "The Lord is just! He is my Rock! There is nothing but goodness in Him!"*

So here we are, each seventy years old, and we cherish each day in the Lord's service and we do not fear the future at all. We are giving the Lord our time and talents. At the same time we are making sure as we lay out our weekly plans while striving to be totally dependent and subject to the Lord, we make sure we take time for ourselves to enjoy life and to spend time together and to exercise and do the "big rocks" rather than just be driven by responsibilities. I did work for fifty years before "retiring" and now am "refired" but living a little smarter, but still serving.

Thanking God

Lord God almighty, thank You for giving us good health and keeping us going. We realize that we only have one day at a time. May we not judge others, but rather spend our days being fruitful through the grace of Jesus Christ and being willing to keep sharing and serving.

We know that Your grace extends for us to enjoy life also. We thank You for men like Caleb, who at the age of 85 said, "Let's take the land". May we not lose the ideal of pressing on to the high calling in Jesus to that final finish..

Dear Father in heaven, thank You for all the times You have brought Donna and me through difficult times of finance and family. Thank You for answering prayers. Thank You for second chances. Thank You for restoring and showing mercy. May we in turn show mercy and help to others as You have told us. We give You the glory indeed.

Lord we pray for those who are struggling right now to find strength in You. May they let others know of the need and may those who are walking in Your love help. Please continue to refine us for Your ultimate glory Lord. In Jesus' name. Amen.

18. Home free ... The Ultimate Goal (Heaven)

"For the Lord Himself will come down from heaven with a commanding shout, with the call of the archangel, and with the trumpet call of God. First, all the Christians who have died will rise from their graves. Then, together with them, we who are still alive and remain on earth will be caught up in the clouds to meet the Lord in the air and remain with Him forever. So comfort and encourage each other with these words." 1 Thessalonians 4:16-18

Heading home –I can only imagine

We do not know for sure what Heaven is going to be like, but we hear the words of Jesus in John 14 saying that Jesus is going to prepare a mansion for us. We also read in Revelation the words of John sharing through the Holy Spirit what he saw of the testimony of the glory of God and Jesus in Heaven. It will be worth it all.

As the song says, "I can only imagine". One thing for sure, it will not disappoint us. We will have a new life. There will be no more tears and sorrows and no evil to harm. The enemy will be destroyed once and for all. The choirs of heaven and the glory of God will surely bring us to our knees and we will live forever. The thought of heaven inspires us to a new height in our commitment to live for Him.

"Since everything around us is going to melt away, what holy, godly lives we should be living! You should look forward to that day and hurry it along – the day when God will set the heavens on fire and the elements will melt away in flames. But we are looking forward to the new heavens and new earth he has promised, a world where everyone is right with God." 2 Peter 3:11-13

Any day you visit the hospital, there are people who may die, and each day the local news lists those who have died. There are many broken hearts of those dying, both young and old. We do not understand, but one thing is for sure: If we are found in Christ and make sure we live so that we are ready to die, we are at peace and actually celebrate the going home.

As the Singer Wayne Watson sings one my favorite songs:

"Home free, eventually, the ultimate healing is to be home free"

Martha in the Bible was upset when her brother died and Jesus seemed so passive. He knew that the life after this life is really a much, much better place to be. Yet loved ones did not want Lazarus to be gone, and Jesus had compassion–he wept–and Jesus raised him from the dead.

May we not dread death, but accept it. We can only imagine how great it will be. I am looking forward to it, I hope you can too! This great and awesome God of ours can be trusted. He will not let us down.

Thanking God and Jesus together

What can we say to such a wonderful God who made us His beloved children through your incredible gift of Jesus?

Jesus, You are all things to us and everything. The Alpha and Omega, and we look forward to that day when we see You coming on the White Horse to bring justice.

We bow our knees to You, Great God, and we come in the name of Jesus to Your throne of grace. It is because of Christ alone that we have this hope of heaven. Our hope is secure as we abide in Jesus our Shepherd and Lord.

Purify and change our hearts O God,so that we might come before you without regrets. Continue to wash us with Your Word and as we confess and turn from our sins by Your power, purify us day by day. Amen.

> *"And the angel showed me a pure river with water of life, clear as crystal, flowing from the throne of God and of the lamb, coursing down the center of main street. On each side of the river grew a tree of life ... Revelations 22:1*

Rounded up in Glory

Throughout the Scriptures, our Lord confirms His heart is to give us the desires of our heart, and we can only imagine what heaven will be like. Surely it would be presumptuous for us to think we could say anything about how it is other than what we have heard in Scriptures and the testimonies of those who Jesus has taken to heaven and who then returned.

There is a book called *Heaven is for Real*, and it is written by Pastor Todd Burpo sharing how his four-year-old son Colton had an experience. It is amazing that anyone would have any problem believing a purely innocent four-year-old who did not even tell a story.

We have a wonderful grandson, Henry, who, when he was four, would utter the most pure observations on life. His quotes came back to us from Rwanda through our beloved daughter Serena, and they are truly amazing.

As adults, we should be ashamed at how much we filter and literally smother our faith, and the faith of others, by our own 'maturity'.

During one of our trips back to North Platte, Nebraska to see my parents, we picked up the book and read it. It was amazing how God used this event of Colton getting sick and actually being as good as dead, but miraculously healed–then little by little over the months ahead pieces of information come out of Colton like "That's where the angels sang" as they drove by the hospital where he had gone to heaven.

Colton and his parents weren't sure what to believe at first, but once they understood what happened, they were amazed that some people would not believe this testimony and cast it off. We enjoyed the book so much, we looked him up and were able to visit with Pastor Burpo at his Church in Imperial Nebraska. We wanted to ask him to speak at our Gideon Convention, but when we heard how busy he was with Colton, we just said, "We will be praying for you."

So what am I saying about heaven?

A few things:

- Heaven is for real. Colton saw it and testifies to how glorious it is. You do not want to miss heaven. Colton is very passionate about sharing Jesus

- Jesus loves the children and so when a child dies and goes to heaven, they are safe with Jesus

- God made a way to get you to heaven, He is doing everything possible to get you there, but we must trust and obey

- It will be beyond your expectations

- Colton had homework. I have homework. I want God to refine me.

- There are horses there. Hallelujah, I will be a cowboy.

By the way, on our trip to Nebraska, we listened to Rounded up in Glory, a CD given to us from a cowboy church in Loveland led by Pastor Greg Deal and his wife Mitzi. They were thinking about how wonderful heaven will be when we are rounded up in glory riding our horses. One thing for sure, Heaven is going to be incredible. God is faithful. He can be trusted. He is our Helper.

I am looking forward to a marvelous time in heaven with a God who understands me, and there is no way I want to have regrets of how I lived, but I want to pursue an honorable life with a clear conscience to God and man from a pure heart.

We are looking forward to seeing you there friend. Thank you for reading and being our friend. God bless you on your journey always in Jesus, Jerry with Donna.

19. Favorite Songs

Donna Kay and I grew up in an a cappella-singing Church and we are so thankful for the ability to sing and enjoy praise to God with the hymns and old gospel songs as well as the new songs.

> *Psalms 150 "Praise the Lord! Praise God in His heavenly dwelling. Praise Him in His mighty heaven ! Praise Him for His mighty works ; praise Him for His unequaled greatness! Praise Him with a ballast of the trumpet ; praise Him with the lyre and harp! Praise Him with the tambourines and dancing ; praise Him with stringed instruments and flutes! Praise Him with a clash of cymbals ; Praise Him with loud clanging cymbals. Let everything that lives sing praises to the Lord !" Praise the Lord!*

My favorite style of music is country gospel and also Negro spirituals which I grew up with, such as "Oh Lord what a morning when the stars begin to fall".

Creation Calls

Morning Has Broken

Do You Know My Jesus?

I then shall live

Hallelujah

Father Hear the Prayer We Offer

Spirit of God

God is the Fountain

These are the days of Elijah

Thank You Jesus for coming to Save us

Heaven's choir came down to sing

Lead me gently home Father

Walking in sunlight

Down by the creek back by the old holler log

Sing to me of heaven

O thou fount of every blessing

You fill up my senses

Great is thy faithfulness O God our Father

Shut de door, keep out the devil

Jesus is my all in all.

I believe in Jesus

Like a River Glorious is God's perfect peace,

My God is an Awesome God,

This is the air I breathe

Grace like Rain falls down on me

Bless the Lord O my soul - 10,000 Reasons

It's a small world after all

Owner of my heart – *(written by Wendy and Bailey)*

Mighty to save

This world is not my home

Precious memories

How great thou Art!

This my father's world

Lord of all Creation

One step at a time dear Savior

I'm trading my sorrows

Light the fire again

Sands of Time

Word of God speak.

O Lord what a morning when the stars begin to fall

Grace like Rain.

Home Free, ultimate healing to be home free.

Christmas Songs:,

O Come all ye faithful

Joy to the World

Silent Night

O Come O Come Immanuel

O Holy Night

A New Song

Godly Men

Let the Walls Come Down

Revelation Song

No Longer a Slave to Fear

We were going to a men's retreat and we needed a good song about Jesus being our Lord, and so Jerry wrote this one.

Jesus Christ has been made Lord
Over all the universe
He is now the King of all peoples
God made it so.

Since He gave His life for me
I will give my life to Him
Talents, Time, and my possessions
Give them in His name

It's not easy for I'm weak
There's temptation every day
But I've found that Jesus delivers
He really cares.

Jesus, Savior, Master, Lord
You are worthy of all my praise
Teach me, train me, as your disciple
Humbly I pray, Humbly I pray.

20. Favorite Scriptures

Donna Kay and I love the Word of God and enjoy spending time each day as we travel through the Bible in a year, year after year. We have never found a mistake and we have never had a day that the Living Word of God did not speak to us.

We do not worship the Word, but we worship Jesus in the Word. We accept the scripture that says all the scripture is profitable and helps correct and comfort. We also believe the Word is as eternal as Jesus and that it makes sense to grow familiar with the heart of God in His Word.

May you also be blessed to enjoy His Living Word and may the Spirit of God fill you more and more and accomplish two things, as Paul speaks in Galatians: what really matters is that we become a new person with Christ in us; and that we become fruitful and pure vessels with Christ in us. May God bless you.

"God forbid that we should boast except in the cross of Jesus our Lord" Galatians 6:14

"What can we say about such wonderful things as these? If God be for us, who can ever be against us? "Romans 8:31

"For we have not been given a spirit of fear, but of power, love and sound mind" 2 Timothy 1:7

"Oh the joys of those who do not follow the advice of the wicked, or stand around with sinners. But their delight is in doing everything the Lord wants, day and night they think about His law. They are like trees planted along the riverbank, bearing fruit each season without fail. Their leaves never wither, and in all they do, they prosper." Psalms 1.

"Anyone who fears the Lord is my friend "Psalms 119: 63

"If you have been merciful, then God's mercy toward you will win out over His judgment against you" James 2:13

Jesus asked "who was the neighbor?" (in story of Good Samaritan) and the disciples said "the one who showed mercy." Luke 10:37

"Give all your worries and cares to God, for He cares about what happens to you." 1 Peter 5: 7

"For I know the plans I have for you says the Lord. "They are plans for good and not for disaster to give you a future and a hope. In those days when you pray, I will listen. If you look for Me in earnest, you will find Me when you seek Me" Jeremiah 29: 11- 13

"The Word of the Lord holds true, and everything He does is worthy of our trust" Psalms 33:4

"Be glad for all that God is planning for you" Romans 12:12

"True humility and fear of the Lord lead to riches, honor, and long life" Proverbs 22:4

"Let the little children come unto me. Don't stop them! For the Kingdom of God belongs to such as these" Mark 10:14.

Jesus said, "I am the way, the truth, and the life. No one can come to the Father except through me. If you had known who I am, then you would have known who the Father is. From now on you know Him and have seen Him" John 14:6-7

"For God so loved that world (that included you my friend) that He gave His only son that whoever believes in Him should not perish but have ever lasting life" John 3:16

"All have sinned, all fall short of God's glorious standard. Yet now God in His gracious kindness declares us not guilty. He has done this through Jesus Christ, who has freed us from by taking away our sins" Romans 3:23,24

"If you confess with your mouth that Jesus is the Lord, and believe that God raised Him from the dead, you will be saved. For it is by believing in your heart that you are made right with God, and it is by confessing with your mouth that you are saved" Romans 10:9,10

Peter said "So let it be clearly be known by everyone in Israel that God made this Jesus whom you crucified both Lord and Messiah." Peter's words convicted them deeply, and they said to him and to the other apostles, "Brothers, what should we do?" Peter replied, "Each of you must turn from your sins and turn to God, and be baptized in the name of Jesus Christ for the forgiveness of your sins. Then you will receive the gift of the Holy Spirit." Acts 2: 36-38

"So now there is no condemnation for those who belong to Christ Jesus. For the power of the life-giving Spirit has freed you through Jesus from the power of sin that leads to death" Romans 8:1

"The Spirit of God, who raised Jesus from the dead lives in you" Romans 8:11

"If God is for us, who can ever be against us? Since God did not spare even His own Son but gave Him up for us all, won't God, who gave us Christ, also give us everything else?" Romans 8:31

"The steps of the godly are directed by the Lord. He delights in every detail of their lives. Though they stumble they will not fall for the Lord holds them by the hand" Psalms 37:23

"A wonderful future lies ahead of those who love peace.. He saves them and they find shelter in Him" Psalms 37:37, 40

"Above all else, guard your heart, for it effects everything you do "Proverbs 4:23

"I have hidden Your Word in my heart, that I might not sin against You" Psalms 119:11

"I look unto the hills - does my help come from there? My help comes from the Lord, who made the heavens and the earth! The Lord Himself watches over you! The Lord stands beside you as your protective shade. The sun will not hurt you by day and moon by night. The Lord keeps you from evil and preserves your life The Lord keeps watch over you as you come and go, both now and forever" Amen. Psalms 121

"God has chosen you to be His special treasure. It was simply because He loves you. Understand, therefore, that the Lord your God is Indeed God. He is faithful to keep His covenant" Deuteronomy 7:6,8,9

Young man: "How beautiful you are my love, my beloved, how beautiful! Your eyes are soft as doves Young woman: "What a lovely, pleasant sight you are, my love.. I am the Rose of Sharon, the lily of the valley" Song of songs 1:15,16 2:1

"How amazing are the deeds of the Lord! All who delight in Him should ponder them. Everything He does reveals His glory and majesty. His righteousness never fails. Who can forget the wonders He performs? How gracious and merciful is our Lord!

Reverence for the Lord is the foundation of true wisdom. The rewards of wisdom come to all who obey Him" Psalms 111: 2,3,4,10

"Then after I have poured out my spirit again, I will pour out my spirit on all people. Your sons and daughters will prophesy. Your old men will dream dreams. Your young men will see visions." Joel 2:28,29

"Is this the one who relies on the Lord? Then let the Lord save Him! If the Lord loves Him so much, let the Lord rescue Him" Psalms 22:8

"A gentle answer turns away wrath, but harsh words stir up anger. Gentle words bring life and health "Proverbs 15:1,4

"God blesses those who for peace, for they shall be called children of God" Matthew 5:9

"As they rode along, they came to some water, and the eunuch said, "Look! There's some water ! Why can't I be baptized?" He ordered the carriage to stop, and they went down into the water, and Phillip baptized him. "Acts 8:36

"Although Abel is long dead, he still speaks to us because of his faith" Hebrews 11:4

"Give your bodies to God Let them be a living and holy sacrifice- the kind He will accept when you think of all He has done for you. Don't copy behavior and customs of this world, but let God transform you into a new person by changing the way you think. Get into the habit of inviting guests home for dinner Do your part to live at peace with everyone as much as possible." Romans 12: 1,2,13,18

"You husbands must love their wives with the same love Christ showed the church. He gave us His life for her. A man is actually loving himself when he loves his wife. Now a word to you fathers. Don't make your children angry by the way you treat them. Rather, bring them up with discipline and instruction approved by the Lord. You wives, submit to your husbands as you do to the Lord" Ephesians 5:25,28 6:4

"Don't be impatient for the Lord to act. Travel steadily on the His path. He will honor you, giving you the land. The Lord helps the godly, rescuing them from the wicked He saves them, and they find shelter in him". Psalms 37: 34,40

"May our sons flourish in their youth like well-nurtured plants, May your daughters be like graceful pillars, carved to beautify a palace. May the flocks in your field multiply by thousands and tens of thousands. May there no breached walls, no forced exile, No cries of distress in our squares. Yes, happy are those who have this ! Happy indeed are those whose God is the Lord" Psalms 144:12,13,15

"Place me like a seal over your heart; or like a seal on your arm. For love is as strong as death, and its jealousy is an enduring as the grave. Love flashes like fire, the brightest kind of flame. Many waters cannot quench love: neither can rivers drown it. If a man tried to buy love with everything he owned, his offer would be utterly despised "

Song of Solomon 8:6,7

"As the church submits to Christ, so you wives must submit to your husbands in everything. And you husbands must love your wives with the same love Christ showed the church. He gave you His life fore to make her holy and clean, washed by baptism and God's Word." Ephesians 5: 24, 25,26

"Don't get rid of doing what is good. Don't get discouraged and give up, for we will reap a harvest of blessings at the appropriate time. Whenever we have the opportunity we should do good to everyone, especially to our Christian brothers and sisters." Galatians 6:9-10

"We are God's masterpiece. He has created us anew in Jesus Christ; so that we can do the good things he planned for us long ago" Ephesians 2:10

"But when the Holy Spirit controls our lives, He will produce this kind of fruit in us: Love, joy, peace, patience, kindness, goodness, faithfulness, gentleness, and self-control." Galatians 5:22,23

"But I fear somehow you will be led away from your pure and simple devotion to Christ." 2 Corinthians 11:3

"Since God chose you to be the holy people whom He loves, you must clothe yourselves with tender hearted mercy, kindness, humility, gentleness, and patience. You must make allowance for other's faults and forgive the person who has offended you" Colossians 3:12-13

"Be even more careful to put into action God's saving work in your lives, obeying God with deep reverence and fear. For God is working in you, giving you the desire to obey him and the power to do what pleases Him." Philippians 2:12,13

"Submit to one another out of reverence for Christ" Ephesians 5:21

"We who worship God in the Spirit are the only ones who are truly circumcised. We put no confidence in the man effort. Instead we boast about what Jesus Christ has done for us." Philippians 3:3

"I can really know Christ and experience the mighty power that raised Him from the dead. I can learn what it means to suffer with Him, sharing in His death, so that somehow, I can experience the resurrection from the dead!" Philippians 3:10

"Let the words of Christ, in all their richness, live in your hearts and make you wise. Use His words to teach and counsel each other. Sing psalms and hymns, and special songs to God with thankful hearts. And whatever you do or say, let it be as a representative of the Lord Jesus, all the while giving thanks through Him to God the Father" Colossians 3:16-17.

"The greatest of all these is love" 1 Corinthians 13 (they live it)

"Sing to the Lord: bless His name
Each day proclaim the good news that He saves.
Let the heavens be glad, and let the earth rejoice !
Let the sea and everything in it shout His praise!
Let the fields and their crops burst forth with joy !
Let the trees of the forest rustle, with praise before the Lord!
For the Lord is coming!
He is coming to judge the earth.
He will judge the world with righteousness and all the
nations with His trust."
Psalms 96: 2 11-12

"But David found strength in the Lord" 1 Samuel 30:6

"Bless us indeed Lord. Oh that You would bless our children and grandchildren indeed, and enlarge their territories, that Your hand would be with them, and that You would keep them from evil, and that they might not cause pain" *1 Chronicles 4:9*

"Always be full of the joy of the Lord, I say it again – rejoice!" Philippians 4:4

"Christ is the visible image of the invisible God. He existed before God made anything at all and is supreme over all creation." "So wherever we go, we tell everyone about Christ.. we depend on Christ's mighty power that works within us." Colossians 1:15,28

"True humility and fear of the Lord lead to riches, honor, and long life "Proverbs 22:4

"O Lord, our Lord, the majesty of Your name fills the earth! Your glory is higher than the heavens. You have taught children and nursing infants to give you praise." Psalms 8:1

"Even in old age they will produce fruit, they will remain vital and green. They will

declare "The Lord is just! He is my Rock! There is nothing but goodness in Him!" Psalms 92:14,15

"Dear brothers and sisters, whenever trouble comes your way, let it be an opportunity for joy. For when your faith is tested, your endurance has a chance to grow. So let it grow, for when your endurance is fully developed, you will be strong in character and ready for anything." James 1:2-4

"Give your burdens to the Lord, and He will take care of you. He will not permit the godly to slip and fall." Psalms 55:22

21. Favorite camping and jeeping

Camping and jeeping ... mountains

God helped us a lot on our trips in the mountains. He is so faithful. One of our favorite roads is Last Dollar between Dallas Divide out of Ridgeway and Telluride. It is a beautiful drive. We were coming down off the pass and the road was muddy and we were on a ledge, the Explorer slipped and I corrected the SUV—actually, we believe God's angels again kept us safe, rescuing us from a fall.

A few of Jerry and Donna's favorite camping spots

- Ouray Colorado, campsite above the town
- Tunnel camp ground on Laramie River Road
- Bogan Flats was our first camp site in Colorado
- Grandview on Long Draw when open to campers
- Brainerd Lake above Ward beautiful setting
- Snowy Range out of Laramie Wyoming
- Teton National Park near Yellowstone
- Red Feather Lakes, Dowd Lake
- Lakeview off Taylor Reservoir
- Lake Irwin above Crested Butte
- Grand Mesa
- Colorado Monument
- Wild Rivers near Taos New Mexico
- Zion National Park
- North Rim of Grand Canyon
- Rocky Mountain National Park
- Anywhere along the Laramie River off Hwy 14
- Favorite is a view, a mountain stream or a lake

It is a little bit hard nowadays to camp since much of it is reserved ahead of time–as much as six months. So if you want a good camp site, you have to plan and prepare well ahead of time.

Jerry's advice for jeeping in mountains

Try to get advice from locals before taking on unknown trails. Sometimes it is hard to find a place to turn around.

It is best to keep a large Colorado map for clarification and compass. It is also vital to have water, and rain jackets, and certainly a full tank of gas.

The jeep trails are rated: 2 is safe for normal car, 3-4-5 increasing difficulty (either distance, steepness, or roughness). You should have a full tank of gas and realize jeep roads can take a lot of time driving 5-10 m.p.h. Be back before nightfall, but always be prepared to stay the night if need be.

Jerry and Donna's favorite jeeping trails

Here is my attempt to list some of our Donna's favorite jeep trails.

Southwest – West

- Engineer Pass (between Ouray and Lake City) 2-3
- Cinnamon Pass (between Lake City and Silverton) 2-3
- California and Corkscrew (Silverton to pass, back to Ouray) 3-4
- Stony Pass (from Creede to Silverton) 2-4 crossing river
- Last Dollar Road (from Dallas Divide to Telluride) 2-3
- Black Bear (Ouray to Telluride, only with expert) 5
- Dubois (east of Grand Junction to Dubois west to wild horses) 2-3
- Grand Mesa (look for south side of Mesa road going down west) 2
- Canyons out of Montrose and Delta 2-4

North Pole Peak off Last Dollar Road

Nothing like taking the back roads of Colorado

Central

- Cumberland Pass (from Cottonwood, Taylor Basin to Tincup) 2
- Paradise Divide (north of Crested Butte first left up Slate Creek rd to top) 2-3-4 WOW !!
- Cottonwood Pass into the Taylor basin (west of Buena Vista)
- Independence and McClure beautiful 2 -3
- Mosquito pass (from Alma near Fairplay go west to Leadville) 3-4
- Georgia Pass (east of Fairplay we did south side) 3
- Slumgullion Pass (out of Lake City) 2
- Road from Paonia south through Crawford to Blue Mesa 2
- Kebler and Ohio (both great with some off roads Lake Irwin) 2-3
- Pikes Peak (14,000 feet day trip good road, have jackets) 2 -3
- Mount Evans (14,000 feet day trip good road, have jackets) 2 -3
- Phantom Canyon (Cripple Creek and south to Royal Gorge) 2-3
- Rye to Westcliff and San de Cristos (pretty rough roads) 2
- Buffalo Pass up north central is fine with some off roads 2
- Trail Ridge (always have jackets for weather change) 2-3

Rollins Pass, we drove it in winter storm 1965

Front Range

- Snowy Range in southern Wyoming a favorite day trip 2
- Baker pass, Jacks Gulch (2 mi past Cameron Pass, Michigan river, Teller City) 3 wonderful trail access at end
- Deadman Pass (Red Feather, take time to go to lookout.) 2 -3
- Laramie River (before Cameron pass go north) 2
- Brainerd Lake Indian Peaks (out of Lyons and south on Hwy 72 above Ward) 2 -3 many good hiking trails
- Pennock Pass (Masonville west over Pass to Pingree) 2-3
- Caribou (out of Netherland, road south Eldora bushes scratch) 2-3
- Rollins Pass out of Rollinsville (no longer can get through) 2
- Eldora to Arapahoe trail (great hike at end) 2

We were jeeping on Last Dollar Road between Dallas Divide and Telluride

On one of our family trips to Ouray with Isaac, Serena, and Henry, Isaac was driving the Envoy and I was riding shotgun. We had Christian music playing, and Henry was in the back seat watching the water cups with straws in the front counsel, and he said, “Hey look, Dad, even the straws are dancing to the Lord.”

There is nothing like being in the high country of God and being able to rest in the beauty of the trees, the wonderful fragrance, the freshness, the flowers, the sound and mist of a mountain stream, and soaking your feet in it and giving glory to God who created it all. Praise His name.

Kyle and Margie with Ruby and Gpa and Gma

This was a very special time with Kyle and Margie high above Ouray where we rented a large log cabin home. It was the first week of October and we were afraid we missed the colors.

However, God blessed us with a week where we actually saw colors changing all week. The weather was comfortable, and we saw a bear and its cub on a drive up CR 5 behind Ridgeway.

We also got to swim in the wonderful hot springs pool. We were able to burn lots of wood in fireplace and enjoy excellent food. On Thursday night, a storm came and dropped several inches of snow, It was beautiful.

During the night, at about 2:00 a.m., I woke up and there was no electricity so I got up and started a big fire in fireplace and lit candles I had brought and got out the flashlights. Electricity was back on in the morning.

Wendy and Jack with Bryce, Bailey, Amber, Ryker

The picture above was one of the times we went to Ouray with the English family–so much fun. This picture was taken on CR 5 behind Ridgeway.

The Lord bless you as you build memories with your family and may you take time to enjoy life and enjoy the creation of God in it's glory. As the song "Creation calls" speaks ..

"How can they say there is no God when all of creation calls "

One of our traditions on our mountain trips was to take a watermelon and stop somewhere and have a party. With all the seeds we spit up there, don't be surprised to see watermelons growing in abundance across Colorado.

Happy Trails to you until we meet again, maybe on some mountain road or maybe on the trails above "rounded up in glory". God willing, we can enjoy many more trips to the mountains before we go to the beautiful mountains in heaven. God bless you all.

Our love to you, Jerry and Donna Kay Swanson

"Jesus went upon the mountainside and sat down to teach them" Matthew 5

Thank you

Thank You Heavenly Father who has helped us for fifty years together. Thank You, Jesus Christ,who helps as our Savior, Shepherd, Teacher, and King. Thank You, Holy Spirit, who helps with power, love, joy, peace, wisdom.

Thanks to my beloved wife Donna Kay who always stands by me, as we live our life together day by day: depending on God together, thanking and praising God together (many times in song), and staying on God's path together. Thank you my treasured love. Your man forever, Jerry.

Thank you to our cherished treasures, our faithful family who inspire us!

Thanks to our beloved adult children who inspire us, refresh us and help us: Cherri and Rich Houle, Wendy and Jack English, Serena and Isaac Tyrrell, Kyle and Margie Swanson; also Erin and Christian Gauthier.

Thank you to our incredible grandchildren who encourage us and delight us: Benjamin, Ryker, Hannah, Amber, Caris, Bailey, Bryce, Glory, Henry, very precious Ruby and Luke ; also Rachel, JoAnna, Bethany, and little Sarah.

Thanks to Caris for the shout out and encouragement.

Thank you to honorable friends who supported us. We thank Dennis and Leala Carlin with Nation to Nation Ministry. Donna Schlachter who did editing. Ken Hoornbeek, good friend, who with his wisdom is helping me publish.

Special thanks to the Heisers who provided us a good place to stay. We have been blessed with so many friends. Lord please bless them back.

Special thanks to Richard and Mark Dykstra and Kevin and Kimberly LeMasters for helping us re-fire.

Thank you to Bob McDonnell for encouragement-comments.

Thanks to Kelli Couch, partner in Real Estate, and Brad Tuttle. Thanks to Bob Tholl and Ron Damon, men's group and prison ministry. Thanks to Gary and Joyce Goulet who brought us back to Colorado 22 years ago.

Thanks to Don and Maxine Hunter, in the Gideon ministry, and so many that we have worked with and become family with in this ministry.

So many precious brothers and sisters in Christ Jesus at our home church, and other churches, all for Jesus and His glory.

Lord, please help us all to live honorably through Jesus.

Thank you Jesus.

"Now may the God of hope fill you with all joy and peace in believing, so that by the power of the Holy Spirit you may abound in hope "

Romans 15:13

This is a favorite scripture of our Pastor Kent, and I share it also as a top favorite. It is our prayer for you as a the reader.

God bless you all in Jesus name,

Jerry with Donna

Made in the USA
Columbia, SC
28 August 2022

65601253R10115